The
Young Republic

The
Young Republic

Michael Weber

RAINTREE
STECK-VAUGHN
PUBLISHERS

A Harcourt Company

Austin · New York
www.steck-vaughn.com

Published by Raintree Steck-Vaughn Publishers, an imprint of Steck-Vaughn Company

Developed by Discovery Books
Editor: Sabrina Crewe
Designer: Sabine Beaupré
Maps: Stefan Chabluk

Raintree Steck-Vaughn Publishers Staff
Publishing Director: Walter Kossmann
Project Manager: Joyce Spicer
Editor: Shirley Shalit
Electronic Production: Scott Melcer

Consultant Andrew Frank, California State University, Los Angeles

Library of Congress Cataloging-in-Publication Data
Weber, Michael, 1945-
    The young republic / Michael Weber.
       p.   cm. -- (The making of America)
    Includes bibliographical references and index.
    ISBN: 0–8172–5703–9
       1. United States — History — Revolution, 1775-1783 — Juvenile literature.
    2. United States — History — 1783-1815 — Juvenile literature.   3. United States —
    History — War of 1812 — Juvenile literature.   I. Title. II. Making of America (Austin, Tex.)
    E301.W34   2000
    973—dc 21
                                                    99–055986
Printed and bound in the United States of America
1 2 3 4 5 6 7 8 9 0 IP 04 03 02 01 00 99

Acknowledgments
Cover The New-York Historical Society; pp. 7, 10, 12 The Granger Collection; pp. 15, 17 Corbis; p. 19 The Granger Collection; p. 22 Corbis; pp. 25, 27, 30, 33 The Granger Collection; p. 34 Corbis; p. 36 The Granger Collection; p. 38 Corbis; pp. 41, 42, 44, 46, 48, 49, 52 The Granger Collection; p. 54 Corbis; p. 55 The Granger Collection; p. 58 Corbis; pp. 61, 64 The Granger Collection; pp. 66, 67 Corbis; pp. 69, 70, 71 The Granger Collection; p. 73 Corbis; p. 76 The Granger Collection; p. 78 Corbis; pp. 80, 81, 82, 83, 84, 85 The Granger Collection.

Cover illustration: George Washington is inaugurated as the the first president of the United States of America at Federal Hall, New York, on April 30, 1789.

Contents

Introduction 6

1. Troubled Times 8

2. The Constitution 16

3. The New Government 27

4. Problems at Home and Abroad 35

5. The Political Parties 47

6. President Jefferson 57

7. The War of 1812 68

8. A Changing America 81

Conclusion 87

Glossary 88

Time Line 90

Further Reading and Websites 92

Bibliography 93

Index 94

Introduction

In 1783, the United States was a new country. It had fought a long war with Britain to gain its independence. That was the war of the American Revolution, which was ended by the 1783 Treaty of Paris.

The United States was huge in territory, larger than any European nation except Russia. It consisted of about 865,000 square miles (2,240,000 sq km). The country stretched from the Atlantic Ocean in the east to the Mississippi River in the west. It ran from the British possession of Canada in the North down to the Spanish possession of Florida in the south.

But the United States was small in population. There were only about 3.9 million people living there when the population was counted in 1790, not including Native Americans. The number does include about 700,000 black slaves and 60,000 free blacks. More than 94 percent of the slaves lived in the South. There were probably a few hundred thousand Native Americans in the United States at the time. Most of them lived west of the Appalachian Mountains, with some in Georgia and North Carolina.

The United States was almost entirely rural. Only two cities—Philadelphia and New York—had populations of more than 25,000 people. Since most Americans lived on farms, agriculture was America's main economic activity. Tobacco, wheat, rice, cotton, and indigo (used for dyeing cloth) were the main crops. Fishing and shipping were also important activities, particularly in the Northeast.

Trade with other countries was vital to the new nation. The United States traded mostly with Britain, France, and British and French colonies. Good relations with Europe were very important. Could the United States win the respect of Britain, its powerful former enemy, and the other

European countries? Could it remain friends with France, its great ally during the Revolution? Or would these powerful nations try to carve up the new United States for themselves?

At home, there were many problems to deal with. The new nation was poor, and it had to build an economy that would provide a decent living for its citizens. The United States was a republic, which meant it was one of the very few countries in the world that had no monarch. Would the American people succeed in governing themselves? What kind of political system would help them do so? Could the states cooperate with each other, or would they fight and break up the country? What powers should the states and national government have? To deal with these questions, Americans developed institutions of government that have lasted to this day.

In 1783, the United States produced few manufactured goods and had to import these things by ship from Europe. Metal products of all kinds, fine clothing and furniture, and glass were mostly imported. Americans in turn exported farm produce, fish, and lumber. But there were far more imports than exports.

Troubled Times

The main issue of the American Revolution had been who would rule America. Once Americans decided they wanted to be independent of Britain, they had to change the way they were governed. Between 1776 and 1780, all 13 states had set up new governments to replace the ones that ruled them when they were British colonies. When the 13 states joined to become a single country, they also had to create a government for the United States as a whole.

The Articles of Confederation

In 1774, before the beginning of the American Revolution, representatives from all the colonies (except Georgia) met in Philadelphia, Pennsylvania, to discuss their future. This group was called the First Continental Congress. The Second Continental Congress, which first met in 1775, operated as a kind of central government for the colonies as the Revolution progressed.

While the states fought for their independence, the Continental Congress drew up a plan for a permanent national government. This document, known as the Articles of Confederation, was submitted to the states for approval in November 1777. The Articles created a new government with one branch, called Congress. It would make laws that concerned the whole country.

Every state would be represented by one vote in Congress. The new national government would take charge of relations with foreign countries. It would also issue money (although each state made its own money as well) and run a national

"Each state retains its sovereignty, freedom, and independence, and every power, jurisdiction, and right, which is not by this confederation expressly delegated to the United States, in Congress assembled."

Articles of Confederation, Article II

post office. To raise money, most governments collect taxes. But the Articles of Confederation gave Congress only limited powers. After being taxed and controlled by the British, Americans did not want their new government to have the same kind of powers. Therefore Congress was given no rights to tax people, and would instead have to ask for money from the states. No national courts were created, and so each state would continue to have its own courts. Congress had no control over the nation's trade, either with other countries or among the states themselves. Each state had the right to make its own trade agreements with other states and even with other nations. The Articles of Confederation went into effect on March 1, 1781.

Achievements

The new national government made two outstanding achievements. First and foremost, it won the Revolutionary War, begun under the Continental Congresses. This was done despite enormous difficulties. Congress had to create and support armies, raise money to fight the war, and unite 13 states that had never before been united. Somehow, it managed to do this. The new United States of America had defeated Britain, the most powerful nation in the world, and forced it to recognize American independence.

Second, the national government under the Articles of Confederation devised a successful way for the United States to create new states that would join the original ones. It did this through a series of laws called land ordinances that were passed in the 1780s.

Land Ordinances

The western boundary of the United States at that time was the Mississippi River. The land west of the Appalachian Mountains now belonged to the national government rather than to any individual state. What would happen to this vast area? The question was urgent. Settlers were rapidly moving into the western lands. Speculators wanted to buy up the

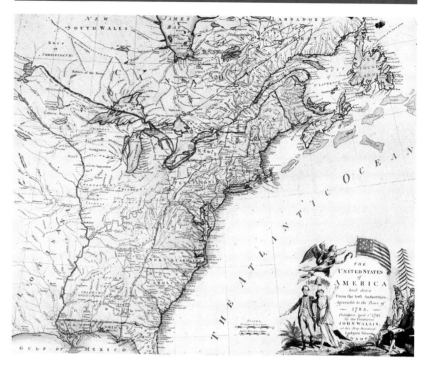

This 1783 map, which is not completely accurate, shows the extent of the United States at that time. The area between the states along the eastern seaboard and the Mississippi River to the west also belonged to the United States. The whole region was known as "the West." The Northwest was north of the Ohio River. The Southwest was the region south of the Ohio to the border with Florida.

land and then sell it to settlers. How would the area be governed? Would it be divided into colonies? Perhaps settlers would try to set up independent nations.

In 1784, a committee headed by Thomas Jefferson drew up a plan for the future of the western lands. Congress decided that the area should eventually become states just like the original 13. First, the region would be divided into townships six miles (about ten km) square. Each township would then be subdivided into 36 sections of 640 acres each, which could be sold for farming. In each township, land would be set aside for public schools. Then, in 1787, Congress passed the Northwest Ordinance. "The Northwest" was the term then applied to the region that was bordered by the Mississippi River to the west, the Great Lakes to the north, and the Ohio River to the south and east. The Northwest Ordinance declared that this region would at first be ruled by a governor and judges appointed by Congress. Later it would be divided into districts. When each of these districts had a population of 60,000, it could govern itself and apply for statehood. The ordinance said that slavery would be prohibited in the new states of the region. (In Jefferson's original draft, slavery would have been banned in all the future states of the United States.)

Eventually, five states were created out of the Northwest Territory: Ohio in 1803, Indiana in 1816, Illinois in 1818, Michigan in 1837, and Wisconsin in 1848. This plan, except for the slavery ban, served as the model for most future American territories and for their admission into the Union as states.

> "There shall be neither slavery nor involuntary servitude in the said territory."
>
> *1787 Northwest Ordinance, Article 6*

Problems with Trade

As laid out in the Articles of Confederation, Congress created departments of foreign affairs and finance, besides a national post office. But it had little success in dealing with problems of foreign policy and the economy.

Under the Treaty of Paris, Britain was supposed to withdraw from the seven forts it maintained on American territory along the St. Lawrence River and in the Northwest. But it refused to do so. The British used these forts to carry on a profitable fur trade with Indians.

Spain posed problems as well. It controlled Natchez on the Mississippi River, in present-day Mississippi. Spain also controlled the port of New Orleans at the mouth of the Mississippi, and refused to let Americans ship their goods through the port. It was vital to American settlers west of the Appalachians to be able to send goods down the Mississippi and through New Orleans. They needed to sell their goods to markets elsewhere in America and around the world. Sympathizers in the eastern United States feared that these westerners might be tempted to ally with Spain to solve their problem concerning New Orleans.

The 1780s were turbulent times for the American economy. In 1784, an American merchant ship, the *Empress of China*, sailed to China for the first time. It carried furs and cotton that it exchanged for silks, tea, and spices, and a valuable new market was opened for the United States. But

11

other markets were being closed. Britain limited American trade in the British West Indies. As a result, American exports of indigo, rice, cured meat, fish, dairy products, and construction materials greatly declined. At the same time, British exports to the United States increased.

Congress could do nothing about this because it was not allowed to regulate overseas trade. Some states—New York, Rhode Island, Pennsylvania, and Massachusetts—put tariffs, or taxes, on imported manufactured goods. But the British just shipped their goods into other states.

Debts and Debtors

Another serious problem was debt. Congress had borrowed huge sums, from Americans and from other countries, to pay for the American Revolution. But it had no power to raise money through taxes, and had to rely on the states. However, the states were very reluctant to provide money. After 1785, Congress could no longer make its debt payments to France.

Many individual Americans, especially poor farmers, also suffered from debt. During the war, Congress and many states had issued large quantities of paper money. This money had lost much of its value, since everyone knew that the governments that had issued it were nearly broke. In the 1780s, several states tried to put their finances in order by raising taxes and drastically reducing the paper money in circulation. This meant people had less cash to spend. Farmers got less for their crops and workers received lower wages. Debtors found it harder to make their payments.

Other states passed laws making it easier for people to pay their debts in paper money. But wealthy people opposed this because they feared their property would decline in value.

Soon, debtors resorted to violence or the threat of violence. The worst incidents took place in Massachusetts in 1786 and early 1787. Taxes there had been sharply raised. Many farmers who owed money lost their farms when their lands were seized to pay the taxes. The jails were crowded with honest men who could not pay their debts and taxes.

In the summer of 1786, a farmer and Revolutionary War veteran named Daniel Shays led what became known as "Shays's Rebellion." Shays and a group of several hundred farmers attempted to shut down local courts to stop them from enforcing the collection of debts.

A Call for Change

Shays's Rebellion and other outbreaks like it were easily put down, although in one clash in Massachusetts about 100 men were killed or wounded. But on top of the other difficulties America was experiencing, the rebellion seriously worried

In January 1787, Shays's Rebellion reached its height when the rebel farmers threatened to seize the U.S. arsenal of weapons at Springfield, Massachusetts. They were fired on by soldiers and quickly retreated. By February, the rebellion was crushed and many of its leaders were imprisoned.

13

Daniel Shays (c.1747–1825)

Daniel Shays is thought to have been born in Hopkinton, Massachusetts. During the American Revolution, he was promoted for his bravery and rose to the rank of captain. Shays resigned from the army in 1780 and became a farmer in Pelham, Massachusetts. He was also elected to several local government positions there. But like many poor farmers at the time, he had great trouble paying his debts.

Shays took up the cause of the many debtors who shared his difficulties. His protests against heavy taxes and loan payments soon turned into armed rebellion. His group was defeated by the militia early in 1787, and Shays's Rebellion came to an end. Shays fled north to the region of Vermont. The Massachusetts Superior Court at first condemned him to death, but he was pardoned in 1788. Shays moved to New York State, where he died in 1825.

"I am mortified beyond expression when I view the clouds that have spread over the brightest morn that ever dawned upon any country."

George Washington, 1787

leaders throughout the country. Many of the men who had led the nation safely through the Revolution wondered whether their new "experiment" in self-government, as they often called it, could survive.

George Washington, James Madison, and several other leaders for some time had thought a stronger national government was needed. Now they resolved to do something about it. As early as March 1785, the idea came up of having a meeting of all the states to consider trade problems.

A meeting took place in Annapolis, Maryland, in September 1786. Delegates came from only five states: New York, New Jersey, Pennsylvania, Delaware, and Virginia. Four others—Massachusetts, New Hampshire, Rhode Island, and North Carolina—sent men who arrived too late. Not even Maryland itself was represented. The meeting was therefore unable to decide anything, but it called for representatives from all the states to meet in Philadelphia in May 1787. Congress backed the idea, and said it offered "the most probable means of establishing in these states a firm national government."

Education in the New Nation

Americans placed a high value on education. American leaders, such as George Washington and Thomas Jefferson, believed that educating ordinary people was important to the success and liberty of a new nation.

However, the national government made no provision for education. It believed this was the responsibility of the local community. Free schooling for young white children had been available in many areas from colonial times. But in the late 1700s, many schools for older white children sprang up. These charged tuition fees and were known as academies. Some of them were open to female students, although higher education for girls was still unusual.

Important universities were founded in the same period, and still flourish today. Among them were Georgetown in the District of Columbia and Williams in New York. Others grew to become state universities, such as those in Georgia, North Carolina, Tennessee, and Vermont.

Schoolbooks, which we now have in the thousands, were rare in the 1700s. But in 1783, Noah Webster, a young New York schoolteacher, published his *Spelling Book*. It removed the *u* from words like *labour* and *colour*, and made changes in pronunciation that set "American" English apart from "English" English. The book became a standard text for schools in the United States, and we still use Webster's spellings today.

Georgetown University was founded in Maryland in 1789 by America's first Catholic bishop, John Carroll, whose statue sits outside the main building. More than two hundred years later, the university is now situated in Washington, D.C.

The
Constitution

All the states except Rhode Island heeded Congress's call and sent delegates to the convention that opened in Philadelphia on May 25, 1787. Over the course of the summer, the delegates—often called the Founders or Framers—wrote the Constitution of the United States. That Constitution and the government it created are still in effect today, more than 200 years later.

> "It [the Constitutional Convention] really is an assembly of demigods."
>
> *Thomas Jefferson to John Adams, August 30, 1787*

The Constitutional Convention

The delegates to the Constitutional Convention were a remarkable group of people. In all, 55 men attended the convention, although not everyone was there at the same time. Most were wealthy property owners. Not one was a woman, a black, an Indian, or a poor person.

From Virginia came James Madison, George Mason, Edmund Randolph, and George Washington. Pennsylvania sent Benjamin Franklin, Gouverneur Morris, and James Wilson. Alexander Hamilton came from New York. Among the delegates from Massachusetts were Elbridge Gerry and Rufus King. Roger Sherman and Oliver Ellsworth came from Connecticut. Charles Cotesworth Pinckney and John Rutledge came from South Carolina. Most of these men would be governmental leaders in the years ahead.

A few prominent people were absent. John Adams and Thomas Jefferson were in Europe at the time, serving as United States diplomats. Patrick Henry, who was governor of Virginia, refused to attend. He feared the convention would strengthen the national government too much.

Washington was chosen as president of the convention on its first day. Each state was given one vote in the convention. The delegates had many heated disagreements. But they agreed to work quickly and in secret.

The Convention Decides

On the third day of the convention, Edmund Randolph of Virginia presented a plan of government that had been drafted by James Madison. Known as the Virginia Plan, it set forth several key ideas. The delegates, after considerable debate, accepted the Virginia Plan. They would not rewrite the Articles of Confederation, as Congress had called for. Instead, they would write an entirely new document creating a new national government.

The respected 81-year-old Benjamin Franklin was the oldest delegate to the Constitutional Convention.

This new document would be the Constitution of the United States. Under the Constitution, government power would continue to be divided between the central government and the states. But the central government would be stronger, one that could act independently of the states. The central government would have the power to raise its own money from taxes, maintain military forces, regulate trade, and enforce its laws.

This kind of system, in which power is divided between states and a central (or federal) government is called a federal system. The delegates felt very strongly that it was dangerous for any person, group, state, region, or branch of government to have too much power. Questions of the proper balance between the states and the different branches of federal government caused the delegates more trouble than anything else. These issues have continued to be discussed through the course of American history to the present day.

"The condition of the United States require that something should immediately be done."

Gunning Bedford, delegate from Delaware to the Constitutional Convention, 1787

James Madison (1751–1836)

James Madison was born on March 16, 1751, one of 12 children born to wealthy Virginia parents. He was often in poor health, but he had a brilliant mind and a good sense of humor. Madison went to the College of New Jersey in Princeton and graduated in 1771. His poor health prevented him from becoming a soldier during the American Revolution, but he was active politically.

James Madison had a long and outstanding career as an American statesman. He served in the Virginia legislature, the Continental Congress, and the U.S. House of Representatives. At the Constitutional Convention, he quickly gained respect as a hard worker, a profound thinker, and a supporter of a strong central government. He took part in all the debates over the new plan of government.

From 1801 to 1809, Madison was secretary of state under President Thomas Jefferson. He was then elected president himself, and held office from 1809 to 1817.

In 1794, Madison married Dolley Payne Todd, a widow. They had no children, although Dolley had a son from her first marriage. They lived together happily for the remainder of Madison's life. When Madison died at the age of 85, Senator Henry Clay of Kentucky said that he had "rendered more important services to his country than any other man, Washington only excepted." He is often known as the "Father of the Constitution."

The Branches of Government

All the states had a government that consisted of three branches: legislative, executive, and judicial. The Virginia Plan called for the federal government to have the same three branches. Broadly speaking, the legislature enacts laws, the executive administers and enforces the laws, and the judiciary settles disputes that arise under the laws.

In every state except Pennsylvania, the legislature had two parts, or "houses." The legislative branch of government was closest to the people because its members were elected by the people of each state. This branch was given the most power.

George Washington (standing, right) presided over the Constitutional Convention. It took months of debate before the delegates finally approved a Constitution for the United States.

The new national legislature, called "Congress," would also have two houses. Here, however, serious trouble arose. Under the Virginia Plan, larger states with more people (like Massachusetts, Pennsylvania, and Virginia) would have more representatives in both houses than smaller states such as New Hampshire or New Jersey. Each representative would have a vote, and so the larger states would have more power in the new Congress.

Delegates from the small states strongly objected to this. After a month of bitter disagreements, a "Great Compromise" was narrowly approved on July 16, 1787. Members of the "lower" house, called the House of Representatives, would be elected on the basis of population. In the "upper" house, or the Senate, each state regardless of size would have two members.

The New Constitution

The delegates moved on to other matters. Many more disagreements occurred, and more compromises were required before the delegates agreed on the key provisions of the

"We the People of the United States, in Order to form a more perfect Union, establish Justice, insure domestic Tranquility, provide for the common defence, promote the general Welfare, and secure the Blessings of Liberty to ourselves and our Posterity, do ordain and establish this Constitution for the United States of America."

Constitution of the United States, Preamble

The Key Provisions of the Constitution

Article I sets forth the structure and powers of Congress, the new legislature. Congress is given broad powers over money and taxes, trade and military forces, admitting new states, and many other things. It can "make all Laws which shall be necessary and proper for carrying into Execution" these powers. The two houses of Congress both vote on laws, but they have slightly different powers and structures. Members of the House of Representatives are elected for two-year terms by the voters in each state. The Senate's members are elected for six-year terms, and originally they were chosen by state legislatures. This changed in 1913 and now the people elect senators. Laws to do with spending and raising money must originate in the House of Representatives. The Senate must vote to approve treaties and confirm important presidential appointments.

Article II creates the executive branch of the U.S. government. The chief executive is the president. He is also the commander in chief of the armed forces. The president negotiates treaties, nominates important officials, and recommends legislation to Congress. The executive branch "shall take Care the Laws be faithfully executed." The president is elected for a four-year term, as is the vice president. The vice president presides over the Senate and takes charge if something happens to the president. Congress can remove presidents from office if they abuse their power.

The Constitution also creates a judicial branch of the federal government. The judiciary consists of a Supreme Court and other courts that Congress may decide to establish. The judges are appointed by the president and hold their offices for life. The Constitution declares itself to be the highest law in the United States.

The Constitution promises the states that they will be governed as a republic, with no monarch. Except in times of rebellion, a person can be arrested only if he or she is charged with a specific crime. The states are forbidden to make treaties, tax imports and exports, or issue money.

Constitution. The finished document was approved by the convention on September 17. Not all the delegates signed the new document. Several refused because they objected to this or that provision.

The Founders made it possible for the Constitution to be changed at a later date. However, they wisely made it something that cannot be done easily. An amendment to the Constitution requires approval by three-fourths of the states. By the year 2000, the Constitution had been amended 27 times.

The original Constitution said nothing about who was eligible to vote in elections. That was left up to the states. At that time, most states permitted only white men who owned a certain amount of property to vote. During the 1800s, states eased their property requirements. Women and non-white men were still not allowed to vote in most states. Much later, amendments to the Constitution changed this.

Slavery and the Constitution

The words "slave" or "slavery" appear nowhere in the Constitution. Yet slavery was often on the minds of the delegates. This is not surprising, as about 18 percent of the population were slaves at the time. Among the delegates, 19 owned slaves themselves.

The United States had proclaimed in its Declaration of Independence that "all men are created equal" and entitled to "Life, Liberty, and the pursuit of Happiness." During and after the American Revolution, efforts were made in many states to put an end to slavery. But slavery continued to flourish in America.

The Constitutional Convention made several decisions about slavery. First, a slave would count as three-fifths of a "free person" when the population of each state was counted. The population count decided the number of representatives a state had in the House of Representatives. Despite the fact that they couldn't vote, slaves and white women were included in the population count.

The second decision was to help slave owners protect their "property" (legally, slaves were property). Congress would be allowed to make laws that helped slave owners capture runaway slaves.

"This Constitution, and the Laws of the United States which shall be made in Pursuance thereof; and all Treaties made, or which shall be made, under the Authority of the United States, shall be the supreme Law of the Land; and the Judges in every State shall be bound thereby, any Thing in the Constitution or Laws of any State to the Contrary notwithstanding."

Constitution of the United States, Article VI

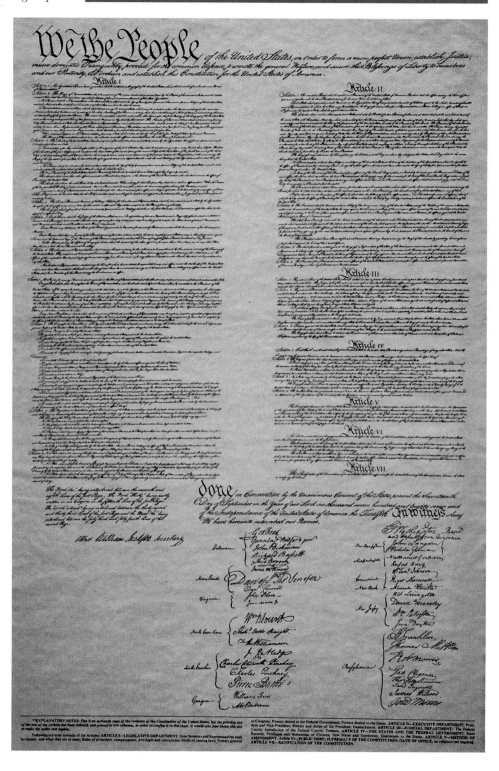

A third issue concerned the slave trade. Several states were still importing slaves from Africa and the West Indies, and some Southerners demanded that this continue. For a time, slavery and the slave trade issue threatened to break up the convention. The Founders then reached another compromise: Congress could not bar the slave trade until 1808.

So the Founders left settling the slavery issue to the future. It would plague America for decades to come.

Checks and Balances

The Constitution strengthened the central government but made sure nobody gained too much power. The Founders built a set of "checks and balances" into the Constitution. For example, a majority in both houses of Congress must agree on a proposed law. However, the president can veto it. But with another vote of two-thirds majority in each house, Congress can override the veto. The president can negotiate treaties and make important appointments, but the Senate must approve them. The president commands the military, but only Congress can raise armies and declare war. The judiciary is independent of both the president and Congress.

Many of the delegates at the Constitutional Convention were slave owners, particularly those who came from the South. George Washington, seen here, was an enormously rich plantation owner and kept many slaves. But he left instructions in his will that his slaves be freed after the death of his wife.

Opposite: The Constitution starts with the phrase "We the People," not "We the States." The Founders wanted to create a government to act on behalf of the people as a whole, not the individual states.

23

These checks and balances work to prevent any branch from totally dominating the others. But, at times, they make it very difficult for the government to solve serious national problems.

Ratifying the Constitution

The Constitution had been written and approved at the Convention. Now it had to be approved, or ratified, by the people of the United States. The Founders realized that some state legislatures would oppose the Constitution, since it weakened their powers. So in each state, a special convention was elected to decide on ratification. If nine states approved, the Constitution would go into effect.

The members of the state conventions were again all white men. But generally, they were more representative of poorer segments of the population than the men who made up the Constitutional Convention. Even so, no women, black people, or Native Americans had a say in the future government of their country.

Throughout the country, debate on the Constitution was intense. Those supporting the Constitution became known as Federalists. Those against it were called Antifederalists.

There were many grounds for opposition. The boldness of the Founders in completely discarding the Articles of Confederation staggered some people. Many feared the new federal government would be too powerful. Others did not want to be governed from a distant place. The United States was a large country, and travel and communications were very slow. Another serious objection to the Constitution was that it lacked a Bill of Rights. This was a statement of the fundamental rights of the people that the government could not violate.

Constitution supporters replied that the major changes made by the Constitution to replace the Articles of Confederation were necessary. They argued that the system of checks and balances would prevent abuses. A Bill of Rights was not needed, they said, since the new government would have only the powers given to it by the Constitution.

"A bill of rights is what the people are entitled to against every government on earth."

Thomas Jefferson to James Madison, December 20, 1787

To support the Constitution, Alexander Hamilton, John Jay, and James Madison wrote a series of essays known collectively as *The Federalist*. The essays were published in New York newspapers and later in book form.

The States Decide

Delaware was the first state that voted in favor of ratifying the Constitution, in December 1787. Within about a month, Pennsylvania, New Jersey, Georgia, and Connecticut also ratified. By spring of 1788, Massachusetts, Maryland, South Carolina, and New Hampshire had followed. That brought the total to the required nine states. But Virginia and New York still had to vote. People believed it was impossible for the new nation to succeed without those two major states.

"The whole of our property may be taken by this American government, by laying what taxes they please, and suspending our laws at their pleasure."

Patrick Henry at the Virginia Ratifying Convention

Alexander Hamilton was one of the authors of The Federalist *essays. At the New York convention, he changed the minds of many people who were opposed to the Constitution. When the Constitution was finally ratified in July 1788, New Yorkers took to the streets to celebrate.*

25

At the Virginia convention, Patrick Henry thundered against the new document for 23 days. Madison defended the Constitution and promised to work in the new government for a Bill of Rights. George Washington was a powerful ally of the Federalists in Virginia. In the end, on June 23, 1788, Virginia agreed to ratify by an 89 to 79 vote.

New York's convention began on June 17. At first, the Antifederalists had a large majority. But news of Virginia's vote made many delegates reconsider. Under Hamilton's brilliant leadership, the Federalists gained ground. Finally, on July 26, 1788, New York approved the Constitution.

North Carolina did not ratify until November 1789, and Rhode Island not until May 1790. But now the new government under the Constitution could begin.

The Electoral College

The Constitution created a complicated method for electing the president. The goals were to make sure an excellent person was chosen, and to give each state an important role to play in the process.

The president is elected by votes cast by the Electoral College. Each state has electoral votes equal to the number of its U.S. senators and representatives. Originally, the Electoral College voted for two people for president. The person receiving the most votes would become president and the person with the second highest number would become vice president. If there was a tie vote, the House of Representatives made the final choice.

But in 1800, two men tied, and the House had great difficulty choosing between them. This happened even though one had been intended for president and the other for vice president. As a result, the Twelfth Amendment was added to the Constitution in 1804. It says that the Electoral College must cast separate votes for president and vice president.

Other changes to the process were made later. Today, the people in each state elect the Electoral College, and the members are pledged to vote for particular candidates. In theory, the president and vice president are still elected by the votes of the Electoral College. But in practice, these votes now reflect the votes of the people.

3

The New Government

T he old Congress under the Articles of Confederation proclaimed the new Constitution ratified in October 1788. That was its last official business.

In early 1789, the states held elections to select members of the new government. Supporters of the Constitution won clear majorities in both the Senate and the House of Representatives. When the presidential votes were cast, George Washington was elected unanimously as the first president of the United States. John Adams of Massachusetts was elected vice president.

In the second week of April, Washington set out from his home in Virginia. He was headed for New York City, the temporary capital of the United States. The journey took him more than a week. Along the way, he was cheered by crowds and greeted in several cities and towns with celebrations and tributes. Washington was inaugurated as president on April 30, 1789.

Washington was not eager to leave private life and take on his new responsibilities. He knew his task would be very hard. But it is difficult to imagine how the new government could have succeeded without his leadership. Most supporters of the Constitution hoped and expected that he would be the first president. This hope had persuaded many people to

The United States' first president was inaugurated on April 30, 1789, in New York City. At the public ceremony on the balcony of Federal Hall (seen below), George Washington appeared to onlookers to be tired and nervous.

vote for ratification. In fact it is likely that many of the Founders had Washington in mind for the presidency when they created the office.

Getting Started

Washington, Adams, and the members of Congress faced many problems. They were very aware that they were charting a new course for their country. Every action they took would be closely watched and might have serious consequences for the future.

Now that the government had started work, the Constitution would be put to the test. But it was vague

George Washington (1732–1799)

George Washington was one of the very greatest leaders in American history. As the first president of the United States, he made it possible for the new government under the Constitution to get off to a good start.

Washington's qualities as a leader had a great deal to do with this. Before becoming president, he had been a military hero. In 1752, Washington became a major in the Virginia militia. He fought with great bravery in the French and Indian War of 1756–63. In 1774 and 1775, Washington was chosen as a delegate to the First and Second Continental Congresses. When Congress decided that the colonies should prepare for war with Britain, Washington was chosen to command the newly created Continental Army. He led the small army to victory against the British.

Washington was not a brilliant thinker or a great scholar. Sometimes he was slow to make up his mind. But when he did, his judgment was excellent. Alexander Hamilton said of him, "He consulted much, pondered much, resolved slowly, resolved surely." He was known as a person of great honesty.

Washington served two terms as president, from 1789 to 1797. He then retired to spend the remainder of his life at his Mount Vernon home on the Potomac River, a few miles from the District of Columbia. Washington died on December 14, 1799. His wife Martha, whom he had married in 1759, died in 1801. After her death, Washington's slaves were freed, as he had requested in his will.

on points where the Founders had been unable to agree among themselves. The precise powers of the president were not always clear. In foreign affairs, for example, the Constitution gives the president the power to negotiate treaties "with the Advice and Consent of the Senate." But what did "Advice and Consent" mean? When should the Senate give its advice?

An episode in summer 1789 shows how this caused difficulties for the new government. Washington was working on a treaty with Indians in the Southeast. He had some ideas about it and wished to ask the Senators about seven specific points. On August 22, he appeared in the Senate chamber with a paper he had prepared on the issue. Neither the president nor the senators were sure how to proceed. One senator proposed that the whole matter be referred to a committee for study. Washington then lost his patience and said, "This defeats every purpose of my coming here." Quickly calming down, he said he would return two days later. When he did, the Senate approved all his ideas. But neither Washington nor any future president ever again went to the Senate chamber to discuss treaties. The Senate only gets to vote on treaties after they are negotiated.

> "[I] face an ocean of difficulties, without the competency of political skill, abilities, and inclinations which is necessary to manage the helm."
>
> *George Washington to Henry Knox, 1789*

Titles and Behavior

Other, less weighty matters also had to be decided. Washington and others wondered about the proper behavior for a president. Should he pay social visits to other officials? Should he receive them at his home? These details may seem unimportant, but they could not be overlooked. As Washington remarked, "No slip will pass unnoticed."

The matter of how the president should be addressed caused lengthy debate. Congressmen suggested titles like "His Elective Majesty," or "His Mightiness," or even "His Highness, the President of the United States of America, and Protector of their Liberties." But these titles made the president seem far too much like a king. Congress decided to call the president simply "President of the United States."

"[My] sincere opinion is that the Constitution ought to be revised, and that the first Congress meeting under it ought to prepare and recommend to the States of ratification, the most satisfactory provisions for all essential rights, particularly the rights of Conscience in the fullest latitude, the freedom of the press, trials by jury, security against general warrants."

James Madison, June 1788

The Bill of Rights

During its first session, Congress took three important steps. It proposed the first ten amendments to the Constitution; it established a system of courts for the United States; and it created the first executive departments.

The absence of a Bill of Rights had worried many opponents of the Constitution. In his inaugural address, President Washington recommended that Congress consider a Bill of Rights. James Madison, now a member of the House of Representatives, proposed 17 amendments to the Constitution. The Senate reduced these to 12, and they were approved by Congress. The states then approved ten of these, and they became part of the Constitution in 1791. These first ten amendments are known collectively as the Bill of Rights.

James Madison's greatest contribution to his country was his work on the Constitution and the Bill of Rights. The Bill of Rights is the foundation for the rights and liberties of every American today.

The Bill of Rights

Amendment I

Congress shall make no law respecting an establishment of religion, or prohibiting the free exercise thereof; or abridging the freedom of speech, or of the press; or the right of the people peaceably to assemble, and to petition the Government for a redress of grievances.

Amendment II

A well regulated Militia, being necessary to the security of a free State, the right of the people to keep and bear Arms, shall not be infringed.

Amendment III

No Soldier shall, in time of peace be quartered in any house, without the consent of the Owner, nor in time of war, but in a manner to be prescribed by law.

Amendment IV

The right of the people to be secure in their persons, houses, papers, and effects, against unreasonable searches and seizures, shall not be violated, and no Warrants shall issue, but upon probable cause, supported by Oath or affirmation, and particularly describing the place to be searched, and the persons or things to be seized.

Amendment V

No person shall be held to answer for a capital, or otherwise infamous crime, unless on a presentment or indictment of a Grand Jury, except in cases arising in the land or naval forces, or in the Militia, when in actual service in time of War or public danger; nor shall any person be subject for the same offense to be twice put in jeopardy of life or limb; nor shall be compelled in any criminal case to be a witness against himself, nor be deprived of life, liberty, or property, without due process of law; nor shall private property be taken for public use, without just compensation.

Amendment VI

In all criminal prosecutions, the accused shall enjoy the right to a speedy and public trial, by an impartial jury of the State and district wherein the crime shall have been committed, which district shall have been previously ascertained by law, and to be informed of the nature and cause of the accusation; to be confronted with the witnesses against him; to have compulsory process for obtaining witnesses in his favor, and to have the Assistance of Counsel for his defense.

Amendment VII

In Suits at common law, where the value in controversy shall exceed twenty dollars, the right of trial by jury shall be preserved, and no fact tried by a jury, shall be otherwise re-examined in any Court of the United States, than according to the rules of the common law.

Amendment VIII

Excessive bail shall not be required, nor excessive fines imposed, nor cruel and unusual punishments inflicted.

Amendment IX

The enumeration in the Constitution, of certain rights, shall not be construed to deny or disparage others retained by the people.

Amendment X

The powers not delegated to the United States by the Constitution, nor prohibited by it to the States, are reserved to the States respectively, or to the people.

For the most part, the ten amendments guarantee basic rights to the people that cannot be violated by the federal government. (Later, these rights were to be protected from state governments also.) These rights include freedom of speech and the press, meaning that people can say or write what they believe. People are free to follow their chosen religion. Freedom to assemble and make petitions means people can meet in public and complain to the government without fear of punishment. The right to be secure means people cannot be arrested and searched, or have their property taken, without good reason. Anyone accused of a crime has the right to be defended by a lawyer in front of a jury.

The National Judiciary

The Constitution had provided for a Supreme Court and other courts to be created. These would form the judicial branch of the new government.

In September 1789, Congress passed the Judiciary Act, setting out a basic system that the United States has used ever since. In addition to creating the Supreme Court, the law set up district courts throughout the states. The states would still have their own courts and separate laws. People would be able to appeal to federal courts on some issues.

The Executive Departments

Congress also decided what departments would be set up in the executive branch of government. After considerable discussion, three departments were created. The State Department would deal with foreign affairs and some domestic matters; the Treasury would handle the nation's finances; and the War Department would deal with military matters.

Later, Congress created other executive departments. For example, the Navy Department was established in 1798, and the Interior Department in 1849. The Post Office became part of the executive branch in 1829. Today there are 14 departments and many other agencies in the executive branch of the government.

Washington's Appointments

President Washington was determined to appoint the best men he could find to head the executive departments and the courts. He also wanted to appoint men who came from different regions of the country.

Department heads were named "secretaries." For secretary of state, Washington chose Thomas Jefferson of Virginia. Jefferson was the author of the Declaration of Independence and was at that moment serving as minister to France. For secretary of the Treasury, the president picked Alexander Hamilton of New York. Hamilton had been one of Washington's close aides during the Revolutionary War and a leader in the fight to ratify the Constitution. For secretary of war, Washington appointed Henry Knox of Massachusetts, who had also served with him in the war.

John Jay of New York was chosen the first Chief Justice of the Supreme Court. Men from five other states were appointed to serve as the other justices. The president's chief legal adviser is the attorney general. For that position, Washington chose Edmund Randolph of Virginia. (At that time, the attorney general did not head a department, but in 1870 Congress created the Justice Department under him.)

Washington began to consult regularly with the three secretaries and the attorney general on important policy

Washington's top advisers first met as the Cabinet when the president called a meeting with the secretaries and attorney general for their advice about a tour of the United States. The first Cabinet is seen here: (from left to right) George Washington, Henry Knox, Alexander Hamilton, Thomas Jefferson, and Edmund Randolph.

33

questions. The group became known as the "Cabinet." This practice, which is not mentioned in the Constitution at all, has continued ever since.

By the end of September 1789, everything was in place. Washington decided to make a tour of New England. The trip lasted a month, and everywhere he went he was greeted with ceremonies and joyous festivities. The new government was off to a good start, but difficulties lay ahead.

America's Capital City

The Capitol building in Washington, D.C.

In its earliest years, the United States did not have a permanent capital city. The Continental Congresses met in various places in Maryland, New Jersey, and Pennsylvania. Philadelphia was often the site. From 1784 until 1790, New York City served as the capital.

In July 1790, Congress passed a law that allowed the president to choose a site for a new capital along the Potomac River. In the meantime, Philadelphia would be the temporary capital. Washington chose his site in January 1791, and work began. The new city, named after the first president, was designed by the French-born engineer, Pierre-Charles L'Enfant.

The government moved to Washington, D.C., in 1800 and has stayed there ever since. At first, Washington was not much more than a little village. Construction of the government buildings took many years. The Capitol building, where Congress meets, was not completed until the 1860s. Before the Civil War, much of the work on the city's buildings was done by slaves. During the War of 1812, the British overran Washington and burned the unfinished Capitol and the White House, home of the president. Today, the city and metropolitan area are home to millions of people. Many government departments and international organizations are based there, as well as important national landmarks and museums.

4

Problems at Home and Abroad

The new government faced a long list of difficult problems. It had to make policies to deal with foreign nations. The needs of American citizens in the West demanded attention. So did relations between whites and Native Americans.

Perhaps most urgent, however, was the need to solve financial problems. The federal government and many state governments had borrowed huge sums of money during the American Revolution. Using its new power to regulate trade, Congress had quickly introduced a tariff on imports. This money was used to pay the government's expenses. But it was not enough to pay off all the country's debt. And the United States had no real system of money that people could trust.

Secretary of the Treasury, Alexander Hamilton, went to work immediately to tackle these problems. He was determined to restore the nation's financial health. At the same time, he wanted to plan for economic growth. Hamilton made proposals for all this in three reports to Congress.

Paying the Debt

Hamilton's first proposal, the "Report on the Public Credit" (January 1790), dealt with the country's debt. Hamilton suggested that the government issue new bonds to everyone who held bonds from the old government or the states. The original bonds had been issued to people who had lent money to the Continental Congress or to the states to pay for the Revolutionary War. A special fund would pay these bonds over time, and this fund would be financed by new taxes.

Alexander Hamilton (1757–1804)

Hamilton was born on the island of Nevis in the West Indies. He moved to New York to go to college, and became involved in defending the rights of American colonists against Britain. During the Revolutionary War, he served as a close aide of George Washington.

After the war, he became a lawyer and a finance officer of New York State. Hamilton was elected to Congress in 1782 and was a delegate to the 1787 Constitutional Convention. He was a strong believer in a powerful national government. Without Hamilton's efforts, it is doubtful whether New York would have ratified the United States Constitution.

Hamilton served as secretary of the Treasury for more than five years. He retired in 1795, but remained in close contact with public affairs. Hamilton had been a bitter opponent of Jefferson in Washington's Cabinet, but he supported Jefferson over Aaron Burr when the two tied in the vote for president in 1800. Hamilton and Burr were rivals in New York politics, too. In the 1804 election for governor of New York, Hamilton sharply attacked Burr and helped defeat him. Burr challenged Hamilton to a duel, and Hamilton accepted. When the two men met, Hamilton fired in the air. But Burr shot to kill and fatally wounded him. Hamilton died the next day, July 12, 1804.

Everyone agreed that the debts should be paid. But over the years, many ordinary people had sold their bonds to speculators. The speculators had bought the bonds for only a fraction of their original value. They hoped to make large sums of money selling the bonds later. Hamilton's plan to pay back the full value would give speculators enormous profits.

This did not bother Hamilton at all. In fact, he thought it was good for wealthy investors to have a stake in the new government. Maybe they would make further investments that would help the economy grow. But others in the government objected to this.

The plan to provide for the states' war debts also caused opposition. Some states, mainly in the South, had already paid most of their debts and had raised their taxes to do so. So Hamilton's plan would mainly benefit northern states that had not paid their debts. And speculators, expecting the bonds' value to increase, had already bought up many state bonds. Hamilton's opponents were horrified to see government policies benefiting greedy speculators instead of the hardworking farmers and laborers who had lent the money in the first place. Nevertheless, Hamilton's plans for the debt and the new taxes were approved by Congress.

A National Bank

Hamilton's next proposal was his "Report on a National Bank" (December 1790). He wanted Congress to establish a Bank of the United States. The bank, run mainly by private bankers, would hold the government's money and do its financial business. It would make loans to businesses for investment. It would also issue bank notes that would circulate through the country as a reliable form of money. The bank would be owned by both private investors and the national government.

Opponents of the bank proposal said that Hamilton was again linking the government too closely to rich business people. They also argued that Congress had no power to create such an institution.

Congress approved the proposal, with most northern members voting for it and most southerners against. The president worried about whether he should sign or veto the bank bill. If it was really unconstitutional, as people said, it was his duty to veto it. Washington asked Hamilton and Secretary of State Jefferson for their opinions.

"The Secretary of the Treasury has declared that these people [the original holders] sold their certificates from choice. A hungry creditor, a distressed family, or perhaps, in some instances, the want of a meal's victuals, drove most of them to the brokers' offices, or compelled them to surrender up their certificates. . . . A sick soldier . . . sold his certificates. . . to a rich [speculator] . . . . Now, can it be right that this poor soldier . . . should pay a tax to raise [profits for] this [speculator]?"

"*A Pennsylvania Farmer*," Pennsylvania Gazette, *February 3, 1790*

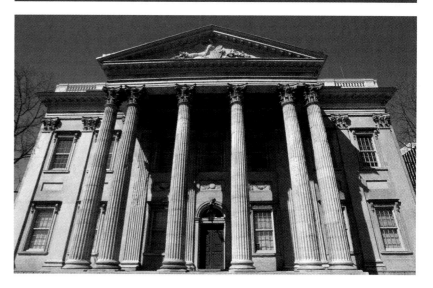

The first Bank of the United States opened its doors in Philadelphia in December 1791. Its purpose was to maintain the value of the nation's money. But its opponents said the bank was unconstitutional and would benefit the rich.

"To erect, and concentrate, and perpetuate a large monied interest, must prove fatal to the existence of American liberty."

Patrick Henry, 1791

Hamilton pointed out that the bank would be very useful to the government in carrying out its constitutional duties, such as collecting taxes and issuing money. Therefore, he argued, the creation of such a bank was permitted by the Constitution. Jefferson disagreed. He feared this reasoning could lead to a government of unlimited powers that would take away people's liberty. Since the bank was not necessary for carrying out the government's responsibilities, Jefferson thought it was unconstitutional. After much uncertainty, Washington sided with Hamilton. In February 1791, he signed the bill creating the Bank of the United States. However, arguments over how to interpret the Constitution would occur throughout the course of American history.

Economic Growth

In his "Report on Manufactures" (December 1791), Hamilton suggested ways to encourage the growth of manufacturing industries in the United States. The country was mostly agricultural and its manufacturing industries were small. Many farm families, for example, ran small businesses making necessary goods like shoes and nails. Hamilton wanted the government to help people starting new manufacturing industries. He also wanted higher tariffs on imports so that American-made goods could compete with foreign goods.

Hamilton's opponents—Jefferson, Madison, and their supporters—were not eager for the United States to become a great manufacturing nation. Even the northern merchants who supported Hamilton feared a decline in foreign trade. Congress decided only to increase some tariffs, and most of Hamilton's proposals to help manufacturing were defeated.

Nevertheless, Hamilton accomplished a great deal. He succeeded in reorganizing the United States' finances, and the federal government gained strength and respect.

Indians and the West

Americans in the 1700s and early 1800s used the term "West" to refer to the vast areas west of the Appalachian Mountains. This included the Southwest (which consisted of the lands on either side of the Mississippi River south of the Ohio River) and the Northwest region.

The Mississippi River was the western border of the United States. The land between the Appalachians and the Mississippi, much of it heavily forested, was occupied by Native American peoples. In 1790, only about 200,000 white

In the late 1700s, Native American tribes and the two powerful confederacies they had formed still dominated the area then known as the West. But white settlers were moving in, fighting with Indians, and claiming native lands for new states.

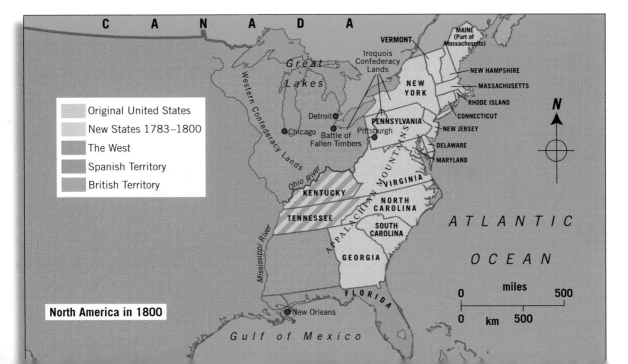

North America in 1800

Original United States
New States 1783–1800
The West
Spanish Territory
British Territory

"You demanded from us a great country as the price of that peace you had offered us—as if our want of strength had destroyed our rights. Our chiefs had felt your power, and were unable to contend against you, and they therefore gave up that country. . . . We ask you to consider calmly, were the terms dictated to us by your commissioners reasonable and just?"

Cornplanter, a Seneca Chief, to the U.S. Government, 1790

people lived west of the Appalachian Mountains. But more and more whites were moving onto Indian land all the time. By the 1830s, most of the Indians had been driven off their lands. These Indians were either confined to reservations or forced to move farther west.

The conflict between Native and white Americans in this period continued a tragedy that began with the arrival of the first Europeans in North America in the 1500s. The whites wanted Indian land, and because they could defeat Native Americans in battle, they got it. In the process, many thousands of whites and Indians died, and traditional Indian culture was shattered.

In 1784, the old Congress had sent commissioners to meet representatives of four Indian nations—Mohawk, Onondaga, Cayuga, and Seneca—from the Iroquois Confederacy. These nations had sided with the British during the Revolution. Threatened with military force, the Indians agreed to give up much of their lands in Pennsylvania, western New York, and Ohio. In the following years, Iroquois were forced and tricked into giving up even more land. By 1800, the peoples of the Iroquois Confederacy had been forced onto relatively small reservations in the region.

Farther west, Native Americans violently resisted the whites' advance. The Miami, Shawnee, Potawatomi, and Chippewa tribes, who lived in the Northwest region, formed the Western Confederacy to fight the whites. They defeated U.S. armies in the Northwest in 1790 and 1791. At the request of President Washington, Congress raised a new army of 5,000 men commanded by Anthony Wayne. Wayne defeated the Western Confederacy on August 20, 1794, at the Battle of Fallen Timbers, near present-day Toledo, Ohio.

The next year, in the Treaty of Greenville, the Western Confederacy gave more of the Northwest to the United States. The land they gave up included the areas that are now the cities of Detroit and Chicago. In return, the Native Americans received yearly payments of about $10,000 from the United States.

The victory over the Indians encouraged more whites to settle in the West. Kentucky became a state in 1792. Tennessee was admitted in 1796, and Ohio in 1803. The Mississippi and Indiana regions were organized into territories by 1800.

The Indians of the Western Confederacy fall to the United States Army at the Battle of Fallen Timbers in 1794. The victory led to the United States gaining more Native American land in the Northwest.

The Whiskey Rebellion

The Washington administration had problems as well with white Americans in the West. Western Pennsylvania was still a frontier region in the early 1790s. Farmers there converted much of their grain crop into whiskey for sale in their region, across the Appalachians, and down the Ohio and Mississippi Rivers. Hamilton had introduced a tax on whiskey that hurt these small farmers considerably. The farmers were feeling a lot of other pressures at the same time. Indian peoples of the Northwest had defeated U.S. armies, the British still held their Northwest forts, and the Spanish were threatening to close off the mouth of the Mississippi River to American trade.

Resistance to the whiskey tax of 1791 was at first peaceful, and took the form of protest meetings. But occasionally tax collectors were tarred and feathered (first coated with sticky tar and then covered with feathers). It was a painful and humiliating process.

After Congress passed the whiskey tax in 1791, there were protest meetings held in western Pennsylvania. People were told to treat the tax collectors "with contempt, and absolutely refuse all kinds of communication" with them. In July 1794, several hundred armed men attacked an official's home near Pittsburgh. In August, thousands of men marched and threatened more violence. Some of their leaders even talked of setting up their own government. This movement came to be known as the Whiskey Rebellion.

President Washington issued a proclamation in August calling on citizens to stop resisting the law. When the rebellion continued, Washington called out the militia of several states and personally led the army of 13,000 part of the way toward Pittsburgh. Hamilton was at his side. The rebellion collapsed without any fighting when the army arrived in late October.

Some critics felt Washington had overreacted. But the suppression of the Whiskey Rebellion was important in reinforcing the authority of the new government. It made clear that if citizens wished to change the law, they had to do so peacefully, through constitutional means, and not by armed rebellion.

Relations with Britain

In the West and elsewhere, the United States faced difficulties with European nations. The British were continuing their profitable fur trade with Native Americans on U.S. territory. Before the Battle of Fallen Timbers, the British had also encouraged Indians to raid white settlements in the Ohio Valley.

Other issues plagued relations between Britain and the United States. British restrictions on U.S. trade with the West Indies had cut off a good source of business for American merchants. The British had also failed to pay compensation for slaves carried off by the British army during the Revolutionary War. Some of these slaves were freed and went to Canada. Others were cruelly resold into slavery in the British West Indies.

The French Revolution

U.S. relations with both Britain and France were greatly complicated by the French Revolution, which began in 1789. This revolution had an enormous effect on world history. War broke out in Europe between France and other countries that were afraid the revolution might spread to them. In 1793, Britain and France went to war. Spain was allied with Britain, and the United States was caught in the middle.

Britain and France each seized American vessels going to the other's ports. Since the British navy was stronger, it attacked more ships than the French navy did. America's trade route to French colonies in the West Indies was especially open to attack, and the British captured hundreds of American merchant ships.

During this war, the British were desperate for men to sail their ships. They claimed that many American sailors were deserters from the British navy, and said they had the right to force these sailors back into British service. On many occasions, British warships stopped American vessels so that their sailors could board and drag off American sailors. Only some of these men were actually deserters. The American public was outraged by this practice, known as impressment.

It was true that British sailors did desert to join American merchant ships, because of bad conditions and poor pay. But by the time the issue of impressment came to a head in 1812, the British had seized thousands of American sailors as well.

Public opinion in the United States was divided by the French Revolution. At first, many Americans supported the French people's wish for a republic. But some were horrified by the violence, and others supported Britain because its trade was so important to them. By 1793, the French Revolution had turned very bloody, and American sympathy declined.

American Neutrality

In April 1793, President Washington issued a Proclamation of Neutrality. The proclamation said the United States would favor neither side in the war between Britain and France. It also forbade American citizens to fight in the war, and barred French and British warships from American ports. A new French minister to the United States, Edmond Charles Genêt, arrived in 1793 to seek American support for France. He took matters into his own hands by employing several American ships to attack British vessels. He also tried to raise American troops to attack Spanish and British territories in North America. After Genêt ignored warnings, the United States complained to France and the minister was replaced.

Jay's Treaty

Seeking to avoid a war with Britain, Washington then sent John Jay, Chief Justice of the Supreme Court, to London. Jay negotiated a treaty in which the British agreed to remove their forts in the Northwest. An agreement about old debts was also made. But the questions of impressment and U.S. trade with the West Indies were not solved. And nothing was done about compensation for the lost slaves.

Jay's Treaty was very unpopular. Many Americans felt it was dishonorable. In 1795, crowds marched in protest and burned images of Jay. The Senate narrowly approved the treaty after a bitter debate. At first, Washington thought the treaty was not good enough. But finally he decided that a less than perfect agreement was better than none at all. Jay's Treaty prevented war between the United States and Britain for the time being.

The Spanish Problem

The United States had still more foreign problems. Spain had maintained its forts in the American Southwest and continued to control the west bank of the Mississippi River and New Orleans.

Washington sent the United States ambassador in Britain, Thomas Pinckney, to Spain to negotiate a settlement. Influenced by the United States' accord with Britain, Spain made a treaty with the U.S. in 1795. Pinckney's Treaty gave Americans the right to ship goods through New Orleans and into the Gulf of Mexico. Spain also agreed to dismantle its forts in the region that is now Mississippi and Alabama.

Washington's Farewell Address

Washington had intended to serve only one term as president. By 1792, he was very tired and wanted to retire to his Mount Vernon home. But one thing Hamilton, Jefferson, and other government leaders agreed on was that Washington must continue as president. So, very reluctantly, he agreed to accept a second term. In 1792, he was unanimously reelected. Adams was again elected vice president.

Within the president's Cabinet, however, policy and personal splits widened. Hamilton and Jefferson had become bitter enemies. Exhausted and upset by the disagreements, Jefferson resigned from the Cabinet at the end of 1793. Hamilton left in 1795, but retained his influence on Washington. The president tried to stay above the divisions that were developing. However, even he was sometimes viciously criticized. Such attacks enraged him. At one Cabinet meeting, Washington stormed that he "had rather be on his own farm than to be made emperor of the world."

"If ever a nation was debauched by a man, the American nation has been debauched by Washington. If ever a nation was deceived by a man, the American nation has been deceived by Washington. Let his conduct, then, be an example to future ages; let it serve to be a warning that no man may be an idol."

Philadelphia Aurora, *March 6, 1796*

After two terms in office, Washington felt he had served his country long enough. He decided not to serve a third term. In September 1796, Washington published a lengthy statement that has become known as his "Farewell Address." In it he appealed for national unity and against the growing divisions among politicians. He urged his countrymen to avoid allying themselves with foreign nations. This advice had great influence on U.S. foreign policy well into the twentieth century.

The Money of the United States

In colonial days, Americans had no standard money. Merchants kept accounts in British currency, but many people actually paid for things using Spanish silver dollars, or by exchanging their goods for other things.

The 1795 gold half-eagle.

During the Revolution, both the states and the Continental Congress issued huge quantities of paper money. But money is worthless unless people trust its value. At the time, paper money only had value if it could be exchanged for gold or silver. Everyone knew that the Continental Congress had no gold or silver to back their dollars, and so the paper money had little worth. It took hundreds of Continental dollars to buy even the smallest things. "Not worth a Continental" became a common expression for something of little value.

In 1792, Congress voted to establish a mint in Philadelphia to make gold and silver coins. The first U.S. silver coins were minted there in 1794, and gold ones in 1795. The silver coins were worth the same as Spanish silver dollars, which were still being used. The Bank of the United States and other banks made paper certificates that were also accepted as money. The U.S. government began to issue its own paper money, known as "greenbacks," in 1862. People now trusted paper money because the government had reserves of gold that gave it real value.

Today's money system has become more complicated. Most countries in the world now use a system that operates on credit and savings and is not backed by gold or silver.

5

The Political Parties

Alexander Hamilton and Thomas Jefferson both had strong opinions about what was best for the new country. But they disagreed on just about everything: the meaning of the Constitution, the role of the federal government, and foreign affairs. These disagreements led to a very important development in United States history. By the time Washington left office in 1797, people with opposing views had formed themselves into two political parties: the Federalists and the Republicans.

Political parties are organizations that elect candidates to office and support certain policies. They play a vital role in America's political system. The Constitution, however, makes no mention of political parties. In fact, Washington and the other Founders at first thought such parties would be harmful.

It wasn't just in government that there were disagreements about running the country. Differences existed in the nation at large. Rallies and meetings were held in the streets to support certain positions and to denounce others. At the time, political quarrels could arouse excitement the way sports events do today.

Federalists and Republicans

The name "Federalist" was first used to describe people who supported the Constitution. In the 1790s, however, it came to mean people who supported the policies of Alexander Hamilton and the Washington administration generally. John Adams was associated with this party, even though

"Let me now. . . . warn you in the most solemn manner against the baneful effects of the spirit of party generally . . . . It serves always to distract the public councils. . . . It agitates the community with ill-founded jealousies and false alarms. . . . It opens the door to foreign influence and corruption."

George Washington, Farewell Address, September 1796

47

Republicans believed that, under the Federalists, the government would become too powerful. This Republican cartoon shows a Federalist journalist as an evil porcupine, encouraged by the devil and the British enemies of freedom.

Hamilton and Adams disliked each other. Washington tried very hard to stay out of party conflicts, but by the end of his presidency he too was close to the Federalists.

Generally, Federalists stood for a strong federal government. They believed the government should be allowed to do whatever was necessary to exercise its Constitutional powers. Federalists also wanted close relations with Britain and disliked France. Their policies tended to benefit banks, shipping companies, and wealthier people in society. There was strong support for the Federalists in the Northeast, especially New England. Rich plantation owners in the South also tended to be Federalists.

Jefferson and James Madison were the leaders of the other party, the Republicans. They opposed many of Hamilton's policies. Republicans feared that a strong federal government would endanger people's liberties. They wanted to leave as much power as possible with the state governments. Republicans believed in strictly following the Constitution. They thought that if the Constitution did not specifically authorize something, it should not be done. Republicans appealed to small farmers, especially in the Middle Atlantic states, the West, and the South; and to working people in cities. In foreign relations, the Republicans preferred France to Britain.

Social Differences

The differences between the parties, however, went beyond actual policies. Federalists and Republicans had sharply opposing views about people.

Federalists thought the rich and well-born should dominate in government. They did not believe that people without property should be allowed to vote. Ordinary people were too easily influenced, Federalists thought, and it was best not to give them too much power. They also said their opponents' policies threatened religion and morality.

In contrast, the Republicans believed a strong government controlled by a few people was dangerous. The top Republican leaders, such as Jefferson and Madison, were themselves wealthy people. But they thought that ordinary people, if they were given education, could be trusted to govern themselves. They claimed that Federalists would destroy the republican principles and individual liberties that were so important.

The place of black people and Native Americans in American society was not a political issue in those days. In both parties, there were supporters and opponents of slavery. Some people in the South supported the Republicans because they feared that a strong central government could interfere with their right to own slaves. The Republican party had good support in the frontier regions, and so it often backed white settlers who desired Indian lands.

Federalists believed that the Republicans would destroy good government in America. This Federalist cartoon makes fun of Jefferson, showing the devil helping the Republicans pull down the federal government.

The Election of 1796

At first, the lines between the parties were not always clear. Local issues could influence people's political loyalties as much as national policies. But the struggle between the Federalists and the Republicans was clearly seen in the presidential election of 1796. It was the first election in which there was a real contest. Washington had been elected twice without opposition. But now the two new political parties presented rival sets of candidates.

Congressmen had meetings called caucuses to choose their parties' candidates. The Federalists backed Vice President Adams for president and Thomas Pinckney of South Carolina for vice president.

Friends and Foes: Adams and Jefferson

In 1776, John Adams (1735–1826) was on the committee that chose Thomas Jefferson (1743–1826) to write the Declaration of Independence. The two men became good friends. They remained so for many years until political disagreements separated them in the 1790s.

In 1796, Adams narrowly defeated Jefferson in the presidential election, and Jefferson became vice president instead. Adams ran for president again in 1800, but this time he was defeated by Jefferson. John Adams retired to his Massachusetts home, where he spent the remaining 26 years of his life. Meanwhile, Jefferson served two terms as president. He left public service in 1809.

In one of the most touching episodes in American history, John Adams and Thomas Jefferson resumed their old friendship in 1812. The two elderly former presidents began a correspondence that continued nearly to the end of their lives. Putting their political differences behind them, they discussed topics ranging from ancient Greek philosophy to their grandchildren. And then, astonishingly, the two great men died on the same day. It was July 4, 1826, the fiftieth anniversary of the signing of the Declaration of Independence. Jefferson, now in his eighties, spoke his last words the day before he died. He asked, "Is it the Fourth?" Adams was nearly 91 years old. His last words were, "Thomas Jefferson survives."

Most Republicans agreed to back Jefferson for president. Aaron Burr, a political leader in New York, was favored by some Republicans for vice president.

In the first election campaigns, candidates did not travel around the country speaking to crowds. The excitement was provided by newspapers, public meetings, and parades.

The 1796 election was very close. Adams and the Federalists won in New England, and Jefferson and the Republicans were strong in the South. The Federalists took New York, while the Republicans won in Pennsylvania. The final tally gave Adams 71 electoral votes to Jefferson's 68. Thus Adams, a Federalist, was elected president, and Jefferson, a Republican, became vice president.

The XYZ Affair

President Adams was soon faced with a crisis. The French saw Jay's Treaty as an American attempt to help the British in their war with France. In retaliation, the French began seizing American ships carrying goods to British ports. In 1797, Adams sent a three-man mission to Paris in an attempt to improve relations. French officials however, would not talk unless the Americans paid them a huge bribe. The Americans refused, and sent dispatches home telling of the French agents "X," "Y," and "Z," who had asked for the bribe. The scandalous event became known as the "XYZ Affair." After this, war with France seemed likely. The president and Congress agreed on extensive military preparations.

The French Crisis

The Navy Department was created and several powerful warships were built. Congress also greatly increased the size of the regular army. Adams did not think that a large army was really needed, but gave in to Hamilton and other Federalists who were eager for war with France. George Washington was brought out of retirement and given command of the army. To pay for the expanded military, taxes were levied on houses, land, and slaves. Republicans

"I will never send another minister to France without assurances that he will be received, respected and honored as the representative of a great, free, powerful and independent nation."

John Adams to Congress, June 21, 1798

51

The Constellation *(in the foreground) was a frigate in the new United States Navy. In 1799, it was sent to guard American merchant ships in the West Indies against raids by the French. The* Constellation *attacked the French* Insurgente *(in the background), and in under an hour forced the French to surrender.*

opposed both the new taxes and the enlarged army. They feared the army might be used to crush those who opposed the Federalists.

A number of battles with France did take place at sea, and the United States Navy performed very well. But to the fury of Hamilton and his group, Adams was determined to avoid a full-scale war. In 1799, he sent another mission to France. The next year, an agreement was reached that restored peaceful relations between the United States and France.

The Alien and Sedition Acts

During the crisis with France, the Federalists, with Adams's reluctant approval, enacted harsh new laws. These were the Alien and Sedition Acts.

Aliens were people living in the United States who were not U.S. citizens. Many aliens had recently come to the United States because of the wars in Europe. Some of them became supporters of the Republican party. The Federalists thought these people might be disloyal to the United States if there was a war with France.

The Alien Act and Alien Enemies Act together gave the president powers to send aliens out of the country, and to imprison them. Adams never actually used these powers. But another law, the Naturalization Act, required aliens to live in the United States for 14 years before they became citizens. This law was clearly aimed at foreigners who were likely to join the Republicans.

The Sedition Act made it a crime to criticize the government, Congress, or the president. Persons found guilty of sedition, or resisting authority, could be fined and imprisoned. In all, 25 people were arrested and 10 were convicted of violating the Sedition Act. They were all Republican supporters. The first prosecution was of Representative Matthew Lyon of Vermont. In October 1798, he was sentenced to four months in jail and a $1,000 fine for criticizing President Adams. As the 1800 election approached, eight editors of Republican papers were prosecuted.

The Republicans bitterly opposed the new laws and said they were unconstitutional. They thought the Alien and Sedition Acts were clearly being used to help the Federalists. The Republicans hoped the states would respond to what they believed were harsh acts by the Federalists. Madison and Jefferson wrote two sets of resolutions that were approved by the legislatures of Kentucky and Virginia in 1798 and 1799. The Kentucky and Virginia Resolutions called for strict adherence to the Constitution and put forth a theory of states' rights. They said that protecting the powers of the states was essential to preserving Americans' liberty. The Kentucky Resolutions even hinted that the states might overturn federal laws if they were unconstitutional. This theory would be very important later in American history.

No other states adopted similar resolutions. But the Alien and Sedition Acts, the new taxes, and the enlarged military had damaged the Federalists' popularity. Republican leaders looked forward to the next election to change the course of the federal government.

"[We] do not wish to invite hordes of wild Irishmen, nor the turbulent and disorderly of all parts of the world, to come here with a view to disturb our tranquillity, after having succeeded in the overthrow of their own Governments."

Harrison Gray Otis, Federalist from Massachusetts, July 11, 1797

The Home of the President

In 1800, toward the end of Adams's term as president, the United Sates government moved from Philadelphia to its permanent location in the new city of Washington, D.C. A competition had been held to choose an architect for the building where the president would live. The winning design was by James Hoban, an Irishman living in South Carolina.

In 1800, when the time came for the move, the president's house had not been completed. But President Adams moved into the cold, damp, and unfinished building on November 1, 1800. Mrs. Adams was ill at the time and joined her husband later. The evening after the president moved in, he wrote his wife: "I pray to heaven to bestow the best of blessings on this house and all that shall hereafter inhabit it. May none but honest and wise men ever rule under this roof."

In 1807, when Thomas Jefferson was president, he and architect Benjamin Henry Latrobe made changes to Hoban's design. The building was not finished until 1833, and has been altered several times since then.

The White House acquired its name after the War of 1812. During the war, British troops set fire to much of Washington, including the home of the president. The building might have been totally destroyed, had not a thunderstorm helped to put out the fire. To hide the burn marks, the walls of the building were whitewashed. It has been called the White House ever since.

The White House in the 1820s.

The Election of 1800

The Federalists once again chose Adams to run for president in the 1800 election. Charles Cotesworth Pinckney of South Carolina was nominated for vice president. But the Federalists were not united because Hamilton and his supporters had broken with Adams over the French crisis. Consequently, they did nothing to aid Adams's reelection.

The Republicans again nominated Jefferson for president, and they backed Aaron Burr for vice president. With the Federalists split, the Republicans' chances of securing the presidency were strong.

The campaign was extremely bitter. Adams bore the burden of defending the Federalists' unpopular policies. Republicans hurled abuse and criticism at him. Jefferson promised to abolish the new taxes, lower government spending, and respect the Constitution. But Federalists accused him of being a godless radical.

The Republicans won a big victory in the congressional elections. They also had a narrow majority in the presidential race. Jefferson and Burr both received 73 electoral votes to Adams's 65. It was clear Adams had lost. But which of the two Republicans would be president?

By the time of the 1800 election, the party system was well established, and so was the practice of political campaigning. This banner used in the presidential campaign carries the words, "T. Jefferson, President of the United States of America" and "John Adams is no more."

The Republicans had intended for Jefferson to become president and Burr to be vice president. However, since each had the same number of electoral votes, the House of Representatives had to choose between the two. It took 36 ballots before the House finally elected Jefferson! Some Federalists had tried to use the situation to keep Jefferson out of the presidency. But wiser men among them, including Hamilton, advised that Jefferson should be chosen.

America's Political Parties

Today, the United States has two main political parties, the Democrats and the Republicans. Confusingly, the Democrats of today are actually the direct descendants of the Republican party that was started by Jefferson and Madison in the 1790s. The other party of the time, the Federalists, disappeared by the 1820s.

In the early years of the United States, the word democrat was often used to refer to disorderly crowds who had no respect for law, property, or religion. Federalists liked to call their opponents "Democrats" to insult them. Those opponents preferred the name "Republican" for themselves. Virtually everyone in American politics at that time claimed they had "republican" principles. This meant that they did not want the country to be governed by a monarch.

Later, the term democrat lost its negative meaning, and the Republicans became known as "Democratic-Republicans." When the Republicans split into separate groups in the 1820s, the most popular group became known simply as "Democrats." Their leader was Andrew Jackson, who was elected president in 1828 and again in 1832.

The main opponents of the Democrats for about 20 years were commonly called "Whigs." That term came from Britain, where it referred to men who wanted to limit the power of the king. In the 1850s, the Whigs broke up because of disagreements over the slavery issue. A new party, calling itself the Republicans, was founded in 1854 by people wanting to stop the spread of slavery. That party has continued to this day. Its first president, Abraham Lincoln, was elected in 1860.

President Jefferson

O n March 4, 1801, at the unfinished Capitol building in Washington, D.C., Thomas Jefferson was sworn in as president. This was the first time the inauguration ceremony was held in America's new capital city.

Jefferson served two terms as president. The next two presidents, James Madison and James Monroe, also served two terms each. All three men were Republicans, and all three were slave owners from Virginia. The three presidents became known as the "Virginia Dynasty."

Jefferson in Control

Jefferson liked to refer to the election of 1800 as the "revolution of 1800." That may have been an exaggeration, but the 1800 election was significant. The Federalists had been voted out of office and the Republicans voted in. This peaceful transfer of power was proof that America's republican system of government was working.

The election of Jefferson and the Republicans was also important because it had a lasting impact. Jefferson was America's great voice of democracy. Throughout his long life, he spoke eloquently in support of freedom and opportunity. He wanted to keep government simple and as close to the people as possible. Jefferson also opposed privilege and wanted to increase educational opportunities for talented young people, whatever their background.

The Republicans' success in 1800 had not been won easily. The election had caused a lot of bad feeling. In his inaugural address, President Jefferson tried to unite the

"Every difference of opinion is not a difference of principle. . . . We are all Republicans —we are all Federalists. . . . I deem the essential principles of our Government . . . equal and exact justice to all men, of whatever state or persuasion, religious or political; peace, commerce, and friendship with all nations, entangling alliances with none; the support of the State governments in all their rights. . . ; the preservation of the General Government in its whole constitutional vigor, as the sheet anchor of our peace at home and safety abroad."

Thomas Jefferson, First Inaugural Address, March 4, 1801

57

country. He was not an effective public speaker, and people at Jefferson's inauguration found it hard to hear him. But his memorable words were printed in newspapers all over the country and made a very favorable impression.

When Jefferson said "we are all Republicans—we are all Federalists," he was appealing to Americans to remember what they held in common. He may have meant that both parties should be devoted to the Constitution. That was what the term "Federalist" originally meant.

Jefferson and the Republicans now controlled both the executive and the legislative branches. They repealed taxes that had been passed under Adams. People imprisoned under the Sedition Act were pardoned, and their fines repaid. The army and navy were reduced, and plans were made to pay off the national debt. Jefferson had not agreed with Hamilton's financial program, but he did not try to undo it totally. Nor did he replace every Federalist officeholder with a Republican. He was not the radical the Federalists claimed.

John Marshall used the cases brought before the Supreme Court to strengthen both the Court and the federal government. His decisions as Chief Justice still influence the Supreme Court today when it is deciding what is and what is not constitutional.

Power of the Court

The one branch of the federal government Jefferson and his followers did not control was the judiciary. Most of the judges were Federalists, and the Chief Justice of the Supreme Court was the Federalist John Marshall, who had been appointed by President Adams.

Marshall served as Chief Justice for 35 years. His decisions in that period greatly increased the authority of the Supreme Court and the rest of federal government. In the 1803 case of *Marbury v. Madison*, Marshall's ruling claimed the Court had the power of judicial review. This meant that when presented with a case involving a law passed by Congress, the Court could decide if the law was constitutional. If the Court decided the law was not constitutional, it stopped being law. So judicial review gave the Supreme Court the final say on which laws governed the country.

The Kentucky and Virginia Resolutions had claimed that the states should have final authority, and so judicial review was a blow to the supporters of states' rights. Marshall dealt other blows in later decisions. He ruled that the Supreme Court could declare a state law unconstitutional.

> "It is emphatically the province and duty of the judicial department to say what the law is."
>
> *John Marshall,* opinion in Marbury v. Madison, *1803*

The Louisiana Purchase

In foreign relations, President Jefferson was at first very lucky. France and Britain were briefly at peace with each other, and so Jefferson was spared immediate conflict. But a foreign problem soon arose.

The 1795 Pinckney's Treaty with Spain gave Americans the right to passage down the Mississippi River and to use the port of New Orleans. But in 1802, Jefferson learned that Spain had been forced to give New Orleans to France, along with the rest of Spanish Louisiana, a vast region stretching from the Mississippi westward to the Rocky Mountains. Spain was a weak, declining country. However, France, now under the rule of Napoleon Bonaparte, was more than ever a great power. What if France would not allow American goods to pass through New Orleans? Jefferson decided to try to purchase New Orleans and West Florida from France. To help Robert Livingston, the U.S. minister to France, with negotiations, Jefferson sent Virginian James Monroe to Paris.

Napoleon had thought of restoring a great French empire in the Americas. But he was soon forced to give up this idea. A large army he had sent to the Caribbean island of Santo Domingo was destroyed by slave revolts and disease. After this, Napoleon felt Louisiana was useless to him. He was also planning on resuming war with Britain and was very short of money. He stunned the Americans by asking if they would like to buy all of Louisiana. The price was $15 million (around $180 million at today's values). Monroe and Livingston boldly agreed to the purchase. A treaty was signed on April 30, 1803.

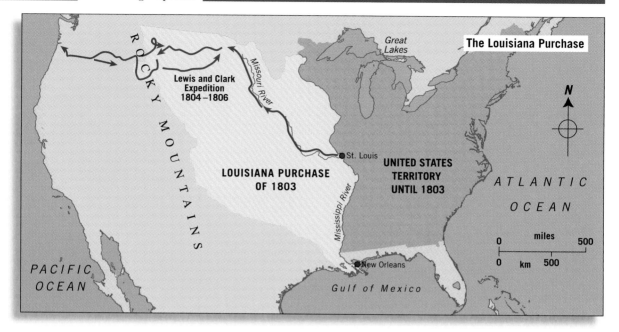

This map shows how much bigger the United States became in 1803, when it acquired the huge region of Louisiana. Over 900,000 square miles (2.3 million sq km) had been added in one extraordinary deal. The map also shows the route of Lewis and Clark's expedition of 1804–06.

The treaty posed a dilemma for Jefferson. He realized the Constitution said nothing about acquiring new territory and treating its inhabitants as U.S. citizens. That is what the Louisiana treaty required. But he also knew he had to act fast in case the impulsive Napoleon changed his mind. The opportunity was too good to miss. So Jefferson ignored the constitutional issues and accepted the treaty. Congress went along with him.

The Louisiana Purchase nearly doubled the size of the United States. The precise boundaries of the Purchase were unclear, which caused problems for the next 45 years. But for the bargain price of about three cents an acre, the United States had acquired what would become all or part of 15 new states: Louisiana, Arkansas, Missouri, Iowa, Minnesota, North and South Dakota, Nebraska, Kansas, Oklahoma, Texas, New Mexico, Colorado, Wyoming, and Montana.

The Louisiana region was sparsely populated. New Orleans was a city of about 8,000 people, and another thriving community was developing up the Mississippi River at St. Louis. But most of Louisiana was still inhabited only by Native Americans.

The Lewis and Clark Expedition

Thomas Jefferson had a keen interest in the huge unmapped area of North America beyond the Mississippi River and wanted to explore the Louisiana region. At his request, in 1802, Congress granted $2,500 for an expedition into the area, when it was still Spanish territory. Jefferson chose Meriwether Lewis, his private secretary, to head the expedition. Lewis made his friend, the frontiersman and soldier William Clark, co-leader. Jefferson wrote instructions telling them to make careful notes about the people, land, and animals of the region.

The expedition started with about 40 men. They left St. Louis in spring 1804 and traveled up the Missouri River. Two years later, the expedition reached the mouth of the Columbia River on the Pacific Ocean. The group had gone up rivers, over mountains, and through prairies and forests never before seen by anyone except the native inhabitants. In September 1806, Lewis and Clark arrived back in St. Louis. They had traveled about 8,000 miles (12,900 km).

Lewis and Clark established friendly relations with several Native American tribes, made all sorts of important discoveries, and sent back to Jefferson specimens of plant and animal life.

Lewis and Clark with their Native American woman guide, Sacagawea, in a 1905 painting by the Western artist Charles Russell.

Jefferson and Slavery

There were already many slaves living in Louisiana. On the sugar plantations that surrounded New Orleans, the slave population was greater than that of the whites. When Congress discussed how to run the new territory, a proposal was made that slavery be barred there. The idea was defeated. However, the law did forbid the importation of slaves from abroad into Louisiana. This ban already existed in the Mississippi Territory.

In 1806, Jefferson proposed a law that banned the foreign slave trade entirely. The ban started in 1808, although it was not strictly enforced at first. It may have prevented thousands more Africans from being enslaved, but it did nothing to weaken existing slavery in the United States.

Before becoming president, Jefferson had tried to get Congress to ban slavery from the western territories. But now he thought (as did others) that spreading slavery over a larger territory would weaken the practice and eventually lead to its end. As it turned out, the spread of slavery into the southern part of the Louisiana Purchase did not weaken it. Instead, it contributed to the coming of the Civil War.

Jefferson was certainly sincere in his dislike of slavery. But he expressed the "suspicion only" that blacks were not as intelligent as whites. He also doubted that whites and blacks could ever live peacefully together. For this reason, he believed the solution was for black people—both slave and free—to be removed from America to the Caribbean or Africa. This view was shared by Madison, Monroe, Henry Clay, and many other white leaders of the time.

Like many whites, Jefferson feared slave rebellions. In the summer of 1800, Virginia authorities discovered plans for an uprising. No violence by black people actually took place, but hundreds of slaves were arrested all the same. More than 30 blacks, including their leader, Gabriel Prosser, were executed. Other rebellions were planned in southern states. A much more serious uprising, led by the slave Nat Turner, took place in Virginia in 1831.

Native Americans

Jefferson's attitude toward Native Americans was quite different. Sometimes he expressed great admiration for their culture, although he felt they made their women work too hard. He believed Indians and whites could live together in harmony, provided the Indians learned the ways of white farmers.

During Jefferson's presidency, laws were passed to provide for assistance to Indians who wished to learn farming. But some government officials cheated Native Americans, and whites on the frontier were more interested in grabbing native lands than in helping Indians to integrate.

The Cherokee people and other tribes in the southeastern United States made a determined effort to adopt the white people's ways of farming and living. But most native societies were not interested in European culture. And if they would not adopt white ways peacefully, Jefferson was ready to have them removed to the distant west. If Indians threatened white people who took their lands, he would use force against them. This had been the policy of Presidents Washington and Adams, and would be true of Jefferson's successors also.

> ". . . They [the Native Americans] have been overwhelmed by the current [of white population], or driven before it. . . humanity enjoins us to teach them agriculture and the domestic arts."
>
> *Thomas Jefferson, Second Inaugural Address, March 4, 1805*

Foreign Problems

In 1804, Jefferson was easily reelected as president. The Republicans had chosen George Clinton of New York to take Aaron Burr's place as vice president. The country was prosperous and at peace. But during this period, the United States did fight a naval war with Tripoli.

Tripoli was one of the small nations in northern Africa, on the Mediterranean coast, that were known as the Barbary States. These countries made piratelike attacks, seizing ships and sailors of other countries and holding them for ransom. To avoid the seizures, countries had to make payments to the Barbary States. In 1805, Tripoli stopped demanding payments from the Americans after losing a battle with the United States Navy.

In 1804, the American frigate Philadelphia was captured by Barbary pirates from Tripoli, and the crew of over 300 men taken prisoner. In a famously daring raid, American Lieutenant Stephen Decatur set fire to the Philadelphia so that Tripoli would not be able to use it to its advantage.

Jefferson's second term was soon clouded by problems similar to those that had tormented Washington and Adams. Once again, Britain and France were at war, and began blockading each other's ports. Both nations seized merchant ships that were carrying goods to the other country or its allies. U.S. ships were frequently seized, and Americans felt this violated their rights under international law.

In addition, the British angered the United States by renewing their practice of impressment. Between 1802 and 1811, the British forced nearly 8,000 men from American ships into British service. The British ignored the American protests. A particularly outrageous incident of impressment took place in June 1807. A British ship opened fire on the U.S. frigate Chesapeake, killing or wounding 21 men. The British then took four men they claimed were deserters from their navy. War between the United States and Britain seemed likely.

The Embargo Act
Jefferson knew the country was not prepared for war. He and Secretary of State Madison decided on a different course. They thought that American trade was so important to

Britain and France that the two nations might make some concessions to the United States rather than lose it. In 1807, Congress passed a law called the Embargo Act to shut down America's foreign trade. American ships were forbidden to sail to foreign ports, and foreign ships could not carry goods out of American ports.

But the embargo failed. Neither Britain nor France felt its effects, and the law caused much hardship to Americans. As was intended, foreign trade dropped sharply. New industries began to produce what had formerly been imported, but they could not fill the demand for goods immediately. In the meantime, prices rose, thousands of sailors lost work, and merchants lost business.

Americans found countless ways to evade the law. Smuggling became a major business along the border between Canada and the United States.

Aaron Burr (1756–1836)

Aaron Burr was born in New Jersey, the grandson of the great religious leader Jonathan Edwards. After fighting in the Revolutionary War, Burr became a successful lawyer in New York City. He was elected to the New York Assembly in 1784 and to the U.S. Senate in 1791. The Republicans chose him as their vice-presidential candidate in 1800.

Aaron Burr was a man of charm and intelligence, but he was not thought trustworthy. In 1804, the Republicans refused to renominate Burr for vice president. He returned to New York and ran for governor. Alexander Hamilton, Burr's political and personal enemy, helped defeat him. After his defeat, Burr challenged Hamilton to a duel, and the two met by the Hudson River in Weehawken, New Jersey. Burr shot and killed Hamilton.

Burr was indicted for murder in both New York and New Jersey. He fled to the Southwest, where it seemed he intended to create an empire of his own. Because of this, President Jefferson had Burr arrested for treason in 1807. Burr was acquitted because of a lack of witnesses, and fled to Europe before other charges against him could be tried. He returned to the United States in 1812 to resume his law practice, and died in New York.

Protest meetings were held, especially in the Northeast. Letters and petitions about the embargo poured into Washington. Many of these opposed the president's policy. Several years later, Jefferson remarked, "I felt the foundations of the government shaken under my feet by the [opposition of the] New England townships."

Jefferson, exhausted and discouraged, agreed to the repeal of the Embargo Act shortly before his presidency ended in 1809. Despite this failure, Jefferson's personal popularity was so great he probably could have been elected to a third term. But he was eager to give up the worries of the presidency, and chose to follow Washington's example.

Jefferson's Legacy

Thomas Jefferson left a powerful legacy. His Republican party, and its descendant, the Democratic party, dominated American politics until the Civil War, more than 50 years later. His belief in a limited federal government and states' rights is still influential today. However, with the Louisiana Purchase and the Embargo Act, he greatly expanded the president's power. His bold actions served as models for later strong presidents.

Jefferson's legacy contradicts itself in other ways. The Republicans were led largely by Southern slave owners. Jefferson's states' rights beliefs were even used to defend the institution of slavery. Yet Jefferson condemned slavery, and believed strongly in individual freedom. His

Thomas Jefferson, third president of the United States of America. This painting, by Rembrandt Peale, now hangs in the Blue Room of the White House.

ideas influenced people like Abraham Lincoln, who were determined to halt the spread of slavery.

Jefferson's eloquent writings on freedom and liberty have inspired the American people and indeed people all over the world. It is this side of Jefferson that people cherish today.

West Point Military Academy

The oldest and best-known military school in the United States is the Military Academy at West Point, New York. It was founded by an act of Congress in 1802. Initially, the academy at West Point emphasized military engineering. The school was small, and the corps of engineers was limited to 20 officers and men. Later in Jefferson's term, it was greatly expanded.

Since West Point offered a free education, Jefferson saw it as a way to help men from poorer sections of society become officers. He also made a point of inviting young men from the West to attend the school. In time, West Point became the leading military school in the country. Nearly all the top generals on both sides in the Civil War, for example, were educated at the academy.

West Point still trains the future officers of the U.S. Army. Engineering and military training are taught along with ethics, social sciences, and management. The Academy now trains 4,000 cadets at a time, and the first women cadets graduated in 1980.

Today's cadets in training at West Point.

The War of 1812

In 1809, James Madison became the fourth president of the United States. He was a Republican and had been secretary of state under Jefferson.

Both Britain and France continued to seize American ships carrying goods. The repeal of the foreign trade embargo did not solve any of the problems with the two European nations. The embargo was replaced in 1809 with a law allowing trade with all nations except Britain and France. When that also failed, the United States started trading with the two again in 1810. The United States said that if either country began respecting American rights, trade would be cut off with the other country. France announced that it would respect America's shipping rights, and so trade was halted with Britain.

The War Hawks

A group of young Republicans in the House of Representatives strongly favored going to war with Britain. Representative John Randolph of Virginia opposed this idea. He called the group "War Hawks," and the name stuck. The War Hawks were led by Henry Clay of Kentucky, who was elected Speaker of the House in November 1811. Another important War Hawk was John C. Calhoun of South Carolina.

The War Hawks represented western and southern states that were not directly affected by shipping violations, but they felt the British were abusing Americans' honor. In addition, they thought the United States could win new territories if it went to war with Britain. Some War Hawks wanted to acquire Canada. Southerners hoped to gain Florida from Spain. One reason was that runaway slaves from Georgia and South Carolina had been hiding among the

Seminole Indians in Florida since the 1700s. Over the years, many blacks in Florida had adopted Seminole customs.

In 1810, Madison announced that the United States was annexing, or taking over, West Florida. This was the region between the Mississippi and Perdido Rivers. U.S. leaders believed West Florida had been part of the Louisiana Purchase.

Indian Resistance

Westerners blamed Britain for other problems. They accused the British of stirring up Indian hostility in the Northwest Territory. But the conflict with Native Americans was due more to the greed of white Americans than to the British. General William Henry Harrison, governor of the Indiana Territory (which was part of the Northwest Territory until 1800), was taking more and more land from Indians.

Two remarkable leaders from the Shawnee tribe tried to resist the advance of the whites. Tenskwatawa urged Native Americans to shun white culture and restore their traditional way of life. His brother Tecumseh tried to revive the Western Indian Confederacy. Tecumseh traveled widely, from Wisconsin to Florida, trying to form a military alliance of Native Americans to defeat the whites.

General Harrison was seriously alarmed by Tecumseh's activities. He prepared to attack Prophetstown, the Indian center the brothers had established in what is now Indiana. On November 7, 1811, while Tecumseh was away in the South, Tenskwatawa led the Shawnees in an attack on Harrison's army. In the Battle of Tippecanoe, the United States forces drove back the Shawnee and then destroyed Prophetstown. The battle wrecked Tecumseh's plans for an Indian confederacy. But Native Americans continued their resistance.

Henry Clay (1771–1852) had a long and influential career in government. His role as leader of the War Hawks was only the beginning. He was secretary of state from 1825 to 1829, and then served for many years in the Senate.

"Sell [our] country! Why not sell the air, the clouds, and the great sea?"

Tecumseh, Shawnee leader

Tecumseh (c.1768–1813) and Tenskwatawa (c.1768–c.1836)

Tenskwatawa (shown, right) and Tecumseh were brothers from the Shawnee tribe. They were both born near present-day Springfield, Ohio. They may have been twins, although some historians say Tecumseh was older.

Tenskwatawa preached that all Native Americans should unite, reject white civilization, and return to their ancient ways. Tecumseh was a skilled warrior, but he was respected by whites for his humanity and mercy. He first fought the Americans in November 1792 and was also at the Battle of Fallen Timbers in August 1794. Unlike other chiefs, Tecumseh refused to sign the Treaty of Greenville in 1795.

In the early 1800s, Tecumseh and Tenskwatawa tried to unite the Indians west of the Appalachian Mountains against white people moving onto their lands. Native Americans led by Tenskwatawa were defeated at the Battle of Tippecanoe in 1811, which set back Tecumseh's resistance efforts. Nevertheless, in the War of 1812 between Britain and the United States, Tecumseh led thousands of Native Americans to fight against the Americans. At the same time, he helped save the lives of white prisoners of war threatened with death by their Indian captors.

Tecumseh was with the British on October 5, 1813, at the Battle of the Thames in Canada. While British troops fell back before an American attack, Tecumseh's Indians stood and fought. Tecumseh was killed.

Tenskwatawa had gone to Canada after Tippecanoe. He returned to the Northwest region in 1826 and then moved west with other Indians.

Native Americans in the South were less united. The Creek Indians were divided between those who wanted to join Tecumseh and those friendly to the United States. In 1813 to 1814, the Creeks fought a civil war. One Creek group was helped by Cherokees, Choctaws, and the United States Army as it fought against another Creek faction. A great battle was fought in March 1814 at Horseshoe Bend, in what is now Alabama. Under the fiery General Andrew Jackson, American soldiers and their Indian allies crushed the opposing Creeks, who were known as "Red Sticks." Creek women and children were massacred.

After the Creeks were defeated at the Battle of Horseshoe Bend, their chief Billy Weatherford made a treaty with General Andrew Jackson which gave the United States more than 20 million acres of Indian land.

War with Britain

President Madison was not a War Hawk. But he had to take into account the feelings of this important group within his party. In early 1812, Madison made one more attempt to negotiate with Britain. When this failed, he reluctantly asked Congress for a declaration of war.

Congress declared war on June 18, 1812. Only days before Congress acted, Britain announced that it would abandon some of its policies that the United States opposed. But the

British would not give up impressment. The news took two months to reach America. When it did, Madison decided to continue the war anyway because of the impressment issue.

The War of 1812

Britain was one of the greatest military powers in the world at the time. But since the British were engaged in a struggle with Napoleon's France, the war with the United States was only a side issue for them.

The United States was not well prepared for war. Under Jefferson, the United States government had reduced the size of the army and navy, and Congress had only recently decided to enlarge the forces again. Moreover, the country was not united. Shippers in the Northeast were making huge profits from the trade that did get through to its destination. They were afraid that a war would reduce those profits. So support for the war was greatest in the West and South. People there blamed the British for the Indian troubles and for low prices they were getting for their agricultural exports.

At the start, Americans thought they could easily conquer Canada. The Canadian population was small, and only a few thousand British soldiers guarded the long border between the United States and Canada. But several American invasion attempts failed, and the British even managed to capture Detroit from the Americans in August 1812.

In contrast, the small U.S. Navy performed well in the war from the start. In 1812, the frigate *Constitution* (also called *"Old Ironsides"*) and other ships won battles in the Atlantic Ocean. The British then blockaded the East Coast to prevent the American warships from sailing.

A United States fleet under Admiral Oliver Perry won control of Lake Erie in September 1813. Perry's fleet then helped General Harrison recapture Detroit. On October 5, American forces under Harrison fought the British at the Thames River in Canada. Tecumseh died leading thousands of Native Americans into battle on the British side. General Harrison defeated the British, but could not advance farther.

Meanwhile, British forces burned Buffalo, New York, in December 1813.

By the spring of 1814, Napoleon was losing the struggle in Europe. Britain was now able to send some of its best troops to America. The British captured much of eastern Maine (then a part of Massachusetts). The Massachusetts island of Nantucket even declared itself neutral in the war. The British further humiliated the United States by entering Washington, D.C., on August 24, 1814. Madison and the rest of the government managed to flee, but British troops under General Robert Ross set fire to the White House, the Capitol building, and other government buildings.

But the British failed to win a decisive victory. Well-trained American troops defeated the British in two battles in July 1814 on the Canadian side of the Niagara River. When the British threatened to invade from Canada, they were turned back on Lake Champlain in September 1814. In the same month, a determined American defense drove the British away from Baltimore.

The Americans scored an amazing victory over the British at the Battle of Lake Erie in September 1813. When his ship was destroyed, the American commander Oliver Perry was rowed to another ship, the Niagara, *and succeeded in defeating two British warships.*

73

The Federalists Protest

Despite the poor American performance early in the war, Madison was reelected in 1812. He defeated his Federalist opponent, DeWitt Clinton of New York, 128 electoral votes to 89. Madison lost only in Delaware and New England.

Even so, Madison and the government had a terrible time during the War of 1812. Income from tariffs dropped off sharply, but Congress refused to vote new taxes. New England was controlled by Federalists, who were against the war and did nothing to help.

Some Federalists talked of breaking up the Union because they opposed the war. During Jefferson's administration, most

> "If James Madison is not out of office [by July 4, 1815] a new form of government will be in operation in the eastern section of the Union."
>
> Boston Gazette, 1814

Dolley Madison (1768–1849)

James Madison's wife, Dolley, was possibly the most successful first lady in all American history. Her liveliness and glamor enchanted everyone she met. Henry Clay said Dolley Madison was "the most charming of ladies it has ever been my good fortune to encounter."

Dolley Madison was born Dorothea Payne in North Carolina. She was raised in Virginia, but her Quaker family moved to Philadelphia in 1783. In 1790, Dolley married John Todd, a lawyer, and they had two sons. But Todd and the younger son died in 1793 during a yellow fever epidemic that swept Philadelphia. She married James Madison in 1794. Although the couple had no children of their own, they lived happily together until Madison's death, almost 42 years later.

Even before Madison became president in 1809, Dolley Madison was the leader of Washington's social scene. During the time her husband was secretary of state, she sometimes served as President Jefferson's hostess. It is believed she held the first official inaugural ball, and began the custom of rolling Easter eggs on the lawn of the president's house.

When the British attacked Washington during the War of 1812, Dolley Madison remained in the White House as long as possible. She saw to it that treasured national possessions were saved. After her husband's death in 1836, Dolley returned to the capital and was active in Washington society until her death in 1849.

Federalists had been against the Louisiana Purchase. Fearing that they were losing their influence, some had suggested forming a separate country out of New Jersey, New York, and the New England states. But nothing ever came of it at the time. Now conditions were different. In 1814, British armies were moving around the country. East Coast ports were blockaded, and the U.S. government was almost bankrupt.

Federalists in New England called for a meeting in December 1814 to discuss the situation. Delegates from the five New England states—Connecticut, Massachusetts, New Hampshire, Rhode Island, and Vermont—attended the Hartford Convention in Connecticut. The convention did not try to break up the Union as some had discussed. Instead, its report suggested changes to the Constitution to give New England more power.

The report also wanted to limit the president to serving only one term, and stop presidents from the same state being elected one after the other. Yet another of the recommendations was to bar foreigners from federal office. This was directed against leading Republicans, like Jefferson's secretary of the Treasury, Albert Gallatin, who had been born in Switzerland.

Despite fierce opposition from the Federalists to the War of 1812, the United States battled for more than two years to defend itself against the British threat. (The state of Louisiana, seen here, was created in 1812 in a small area of the Louisiana Purchase of 1803.)

The End of the War
The Hartford Convention was furiously denounced by Republicans. However, the meeting was largely forgotten when exciting news arrived from New

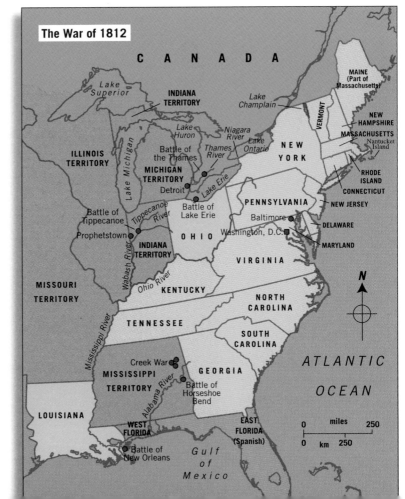

The War of 1812

Orleans. There, at the mouth of the Mississippi River, three battles took place in December 1814 and January 1815.

A large British army under General Sir Edward Pakenham had landed. Opposing it was an American force of regular army troops, marksmen from Kentucky and Tennessee, and local militiamen and volunteers. Among these were the smuggler Jean Laffite and his men, who had expert knowledge of New Orleans's waterways. The U.S. commander was Andrew Jackson, fresh from his victory at Horseshoe Bend.

In the main battle on January 8, 1815, Jackson's forces soundly defeated the British. Pakenham and two other British generals were killed, and the British suffered nearly 2,500 casualties. The Americans lost fewer than 400 men. The battle made Jackson a national hero.

Reports of the Battle of New Orleans had just reached the eastern United States in February when another piece of happy news arrived. A peace treaty between the United States and Britain had been signed before the Battle of New Orleans!

Negotiations had begun in August 1814 in the city of Ghent, now in Belgium. The talks went on for several months. Each side presented demands that the other could

British and American diplomats signed the Treaty of Ghent on December 24, 1814. John Quincy Adams, the son of former President John Adams, led the American delegation, which also included Henry Clay and Albert Gallatin.

not accept. There were disputes over boundaries, the Great Lakes, and fishing rights in the North Atlantic. Impressment was also an issue, and so was protection for Native Americans allied to the British.

The United States was eager for peace, but unwilling to surrender any rights it had won after the American Revolution. Finally, the British also decided that continuing the war was not in their interest. They still had problems to deal with in Europe and financial problems in their own country.

On December 24, 1814, the negotiators signed the Treaty of Ghent. It mentioned none of the issues that had caused the war. But since Britain and France were now at peace, there was no longer any reason for American shipping rights to be violated or for the British to impress American sailors. On February 17, 1815, Madison proclaimed the war over.

The Aftermath of the War

The end of the war and the victory at New Orleans caused a great surge of patriotism throughout America. The United States had again held its own against Britain, the most powerful nation in the world. It was as if a second war of independence had been won.

After the war, some of the old political disputes returned. The Bank of the United States, created in 1791 by Alexander Hamilton, had been put out of business by Congress in 1811. Madison had at first thought the bank was unconstitutional. But now that he was president, he believed a new national bank was necessary to manage the government's financial affairs. In 1816, Congress approved the creation of the Second Bank of the United States.

Madison, like most other Republicans, had also been against Hamilton's plans to develop new manufacturing industries. But the embargo and the War of 1812 had shown that it was important for America to be able to produce what it needed instead of depending on others. So, in 1816, Congress passed a law for new tariffs on imports. This was to protect America's textile industries from foreign competition.

"Notwithstanding a thousand faults and blunders, [Madison's] Adminstration has acquired more glory, and established more Union, than all three Predecessors, Washington, Adams, and Jefferson put together."

John Adams to Thomas Jefferson, February 1, 1817

James Monroe (1758–1831)

Monroe was born in Westmoreland County, Virginia. He served heroically in the Continental Army during the Revolutionary War, and was seriously wounded at the Battle of Trenton in December 1776. In 1780, Monroe returned to Virginia, where he studied law under Jefferson.

Monroe then began a long career of public service. He was a member of the Virginia legislature and the Continental Congress in the 1780s. He served as a U.S. senator from 1790 to 1794. Monroe became minister to France, and then governor of Virginia from 1799 to 1802. President Jefferson sent him back to France in 1803 to help negotiate the Louisiana Purchase, and then to Spain to negotiate the boundaries of Louisiana. Monroe also went to Britain to represent America over impressment and shipping rights.

In 1811, President Madison appointed Monroe secretary of state, and he doubled as secretary of war during the War of 1812. Monroe was then president from 1817 to 1825. In 1823, Monroe proclaimed the doctrine named after him. The Monroe Doctrine was a message to the rest of the world, especially the powers of Europe. It said that the United States would not accept any further colonization in the Americas, nor any expansion of European power. The doctrine also stated that the United States in turn would not interfere in European territories or affairs.

After his second term as president, Monroe served on the governing board of the University of Virginia. He died in New York on July 4, 1831.

Madison's second term ended in March 1817. During his presidency he had been bitterly criticized. But he left office amid the great feeling of national pride that followed the War of 1812. Madison's successor was James Monroe. The

Federalist party hardly survived after the War of 1812. Monroe won easily, beating his Federalist rival Rufus King by 183 electoral votes to 34.

The Era of Good Feelings

Monroe's inauguration began a brief period often called "the Era of Good Feelings." America was proud of itself, at peace, and prosperous. Political disputes were mild as the Federalist party faded away.

To celebrate and strengthen America's feeling of unity, President Monroe decided to make a tour of the country. No president had done this since George Washington. Monroe visited the East in the summer of 1817, and the West and South in 1819. Everywhere he was met by dignitaries and acclaimed by crowds. In Boston, he was greeted by 40,000 people. Monroe wrote Madison that he did not think the demonstrations were meant for him personally. They showed a "desire in the body of the people to show their attachment to the union."

The settlement of long-standing foreign problems helped the nation's good feeling. Two important agreements were worked out with Britain. The first was the 1817 Rush-Bagot Treaty. This was named after its two main negotiators, the American diplomat Richard Rush and the British minister

The Rush-Bagot agreement of 1817 set limits for both American and British naval forces on the Great Lakes, where the boundary runs between Canada and the United States. The Adam-Onís Treaty of 1819 enlarged the territory of the United States. The country gained Florida and now extended to the Pacific Ocean as well. Six new states also joined the union between 1816 and 1821.

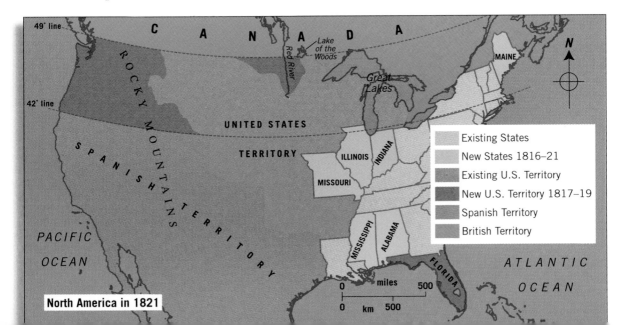

North America in 1821

Existing States
New States 1816–21
Existing U.S. Territory
New U.S. Territory 1817–19
Spanish Territory
British Territory

in Washington, Sir Charles Bagot. The second was the Convention of 1818. These two agreements cleared up disputes over the U.S.-Canadian border and made sure that neither country would threaten the other across the border.

John Quincy Adams, Monroe's secretary of state, made a very important agreement in 1819 with Spain. He negotiated with the Spanish minister to the United States, Luis de Onís. The Adams-Onís Treaty settled arguments about the exact boundaries of the Louisiana Purchase. Under the treaty, Spain gave East Florida to the United States and abandoned all its claims to West Florida. In return, the United States gave up its claims to Texas.

The two countries also agreed on the border between the United States and Spanish possessions in the West. This border extended northwest from the Gulf of Mexico to the 42nd parallel and then west to the Pacific Ocean. It gave the United States a large Pacific coast region. The nation now extended from the Atlantic Ocean to the Pacific Ocean.

America's National Anthem

America's national anthem is "The Star-Spangled Banner." Its words were written during the War of 1812 by Francis Scott Key, a young lawyer.

In September 1813, Key went aboard a British ship to seek the release of a doctor whom the British had captured. He spent the night on the ship as the British bombarded Fort McHenry, near Baltimore. Key was certain the fort would surrender,

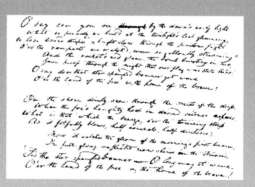

The first lines of Francis Scott Key's autographed manuscript of "The Star-Spangled Banner."

but in the morning he saw the American flag still flying over the fort. He then wrote the words of his song, setting them to a popular tune of the time. Within a few days, the song was widely printed throughout the country. Although widely popular, the song did not become the official national anthem until 1931, when Congress made it so by law.

8

A Changing America

I n 1820, the United States Constitution had been in place for more than 30 years. The government had achieved most of what the Constitution's supporters had set out to do.

A Working Government

The United States had solved its financial problems and kept its independence. It had even held its own in a second war with Britain. The federal government was strong enough to defend the nation's borders. It also used its strength to take land from the Native Americans and give it to white settlers.

There were many disagreements over where the powers of the federal government ended and those of the states began. But a balance appeared to have been reached. Under the federal system, the states still had real authority. Southerners in particular made sure to defend the powers of the state governments.

Within the federal government, the rules of the Constitution were being followed. The executive branch was run by the president and his Cabinet. The system left much decision-making to

This painting shows the House of Representatives as it was in 1822. The Supreme Court and the executive branch both had considerable powers, but the day-to-day decision-making took place in both houses of Congress.

In the West of the 1800s, towns like Pittsburgh (seen here), Cincinnati, and Louisville grew into cities because of their location on major rivers. As farmers in the West shipped more and more of their products to the East and to New Orleans, the towns grew rapidly. And the face of these cities changed as industrialization and factories took hold.

Congress, but the president was allowed to respond to emergencies. Washington did this with the Whiskey Rebellion, and Jefferson did with the Louisiana Purchase. Meanwhile, Chief Justice John Marshall was making the Supreme Court the ultimate authority on the Constitution.

Political parties were now an essential part of government. Parties put forth candidates at elections. The Republican party had elected three presidents: Jefferson, Madison, and Monroe. The Federalist party had disappeared by the early 1820s. In fact, when Monroe ran for reelection in 1820, he won every electoral vote but one. After 1820, however, the Republicans split into factions. There were as many as five serious candidates for president in 1824.

The Cities Grow

The kind of work people did and where they lived began to change. Farming was still America's main economic activity, but the cities were growing. Older cities like New York, Boston, and Baltimore grew as their harbors handled more and more overseas trade. Sometime in the early 1800s, New York overtook Philadelphia as the largest city in America. In 1820, they both had populations of over 100,000. Baltimore had 63,000 people and Boston had 43,000.

The growth of cities took place as manufacturing began to grow gradually in the United States. By 1820, the Industrial

The Industrial Revolution

The interruptions in foreign trade (caused by the embargo and the War of 1812) forced Americans to start making some of the products that they were used to importing from Europe. Most manufacturing was still done by craftsmen and women in shops or at home. But big changes began to appear in the northeastern United States in the early 1800s.

The Industrial Revolution had begun in Britain in the mid-1700s. This was when people began to produce goods in factories. Instead of working in their homes, they earned their living in factories, often using machines.

Between 1815 and 1820, textile manufacturing became an important industry in New England. So did making the machines for producing textiles. Around the same time, the iron industry developed in the Pittsburgh area. In 1817, the first factory for making paper was started in Wilmington, Delaware.

Much of the new machinery used in these factories was developed in Britain. But the United States made an important contribution to the Industrial Revolution. Interchangeable parts are the pieces of products and machines that can be made in large quantities, assembled into products, and replaced when they break or wear out. Eli Whitney, the inventor of the cotton gin, was a leader in developing these parts. In 1800, he was employed by the U.S. government to supply rifles. Whitney devised a method for making them using interchangeable parts. This meant that the rifles could be produced quickly in large numbers, rather than slowly, one by one. It is because of interchangeable parts that we now have "mass production," or making huge quantities of the same thing, in factories today.

Women working outside the home in a textile mill of 1834.

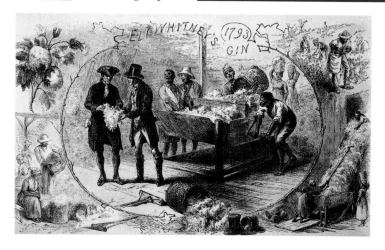

The first cotton gins enabled workers—who were usually slaves—to produce 50 times more fiber than before. Later versions did even better.

Revolution was taking hold. People were finding jobs in city factories, where they produced goods in large numbers.

The start of modern working methods could be seen in other ways. The first American labor unions were being organized around this time. Labor unions are organizations of workers that try to improve wages and working conditions for their members. Printers in Boston went on strike in 1809, and strikes took place in other cities in subsequent years.

Changes in Farming

Agriculture was also going through important changes. Wheat and corn were the leading crops in the North and West, but cattle raising was growing in importance. In the South, cotton and tobacco were the most important commercial crops. The cultivation of cotton received an enormous boost in 1793 from the invention of the cotton gin by Eli Whitney. Separating the valuable cotton fiber from the seeds had been a difficult, slow task until then. The cotton gin made it much easier. As a result, cotton production and profits increased enormously.

There was another, less happy consequence. The growth in cotton cultivation made slavery much more profitable to slave owners, and support for slavery in the South grew stronger.

Banks and Finance

The number of banks in America increased greatly in the early 1800s. The success of the Bank of the United States was followed by the creation of many state banks. In 1791, there had been only three banks in the whole country. By the 1820s, there were hundreds of banks. Banks were needed to finance new businesses and help the economy grow.

Unfortunately, not all the new banks were well managed. In 1816, Congress had created the Second Bank of the United States to be the country's national bank. The national bank and many state banks made some bad decisions that helped bring on a financial crisis in 1819. Businesses failed and many people fell hopelessly into debt.

The Pennsylvania turnpike, seen here in 1795, was one of the earliest toll roads. By 1810, there were about 300 corporations building roads in the eastern United States.

New Kinds of Transportation

In 1800, people could travel no faster on land than horses could carry them. On water, they were dependent on wind and sails. There had been no basic change in the way people or goods traveled for thousands of years. As the United States grew in size, the huge distances that goods and information had to travel caused many problems.

The first turnpikes were built at the end of the 1700s. People traveling on turnpike roads had to pay a toll, and the money went to the people who had paid for the road to be built. Congress authorized the Cumberland, or Old National Road, in 1806, and construction began in 1811. The road ran west from Cumberland, Maryland, and eventually went as far as Vandalia, Illinois.

Shipping goods by water was cheaper than by land. Since the 1780s, inventors had been working on the idea of powering a boat with the recently invented steam engine.

In 1807, Pennsylvania-born Robert Fulton made a breakthrough. Fulton built the *Clermont*, a boat powered by a steam-driven paddlewheel. Steamboats made water travel much easier and more economical.

In the 1790s, canals had been built in Massachusetts, New York, and South Carolina. These canals were all under 28 miles (45 km) long. In 1817, New York State started to build the Erie Canal from Albany to Buffalo. The Erie Canal was completed in 1825, and was 363 miles (584 km) long! People who used it were required to pay tolls, just as they did on turnpikes. Within a few years, the canal was making a profit.

The canal made it much easier and cheaper for farm products from the Great Lakes region to reach the East Coast. Buffalo, Rochester, Syracuse, and other cities along the canal's route flourished. And all across the country, a canal construction boom got underway.

The spread of roads and canals across the United States was the beginning of what is called the Transportation Revolution. America's economy began to grow along with its new forms of transport.

The Expansion of the Union

The United States grew much larger between 1783 and 1821. The 13 original states were joined by 11 new states, and by 1821, the nation's area was almost 1.75 million square miles (4.5 million sq km). The U. S. population nearly doubled. In 1820, there were 9.6 million Americans, including 1.5 million slaves and 235,000 free blacks. About 2 million people (not counting Indians) were living west of the Appalachians.

States Admitted to the Union, 1791–1821

Vermont	1791	Louisiana	1812	Alabama	1819
Kentucky	1792	Indiana	1816	Maine	1820
Tennessee	1796	Mississippi	1817	Missouri	1821
Ohio	1803	Illinois	1818		

Conclusion

America's territory was expanding and its population was increasing. Cites grew, the economy developed, and new kinds of transportation appeared. Society was becoming more complex. These important changes would pose difficult problems for the nation in the years ahead.

Could the balance created by the Constitution between the states and federal government be preserved? Would Jefferson's idea of a limited government in a farming society continue to be workable? During Monroe's presidency, these problems brought a quick end to the "Era of Good Feelings."

What consequences would America's relentless movement west have for the Native Americans, who had already suffered so much? Many more injustices would be inflicted on them in the near future. And what about the issue of slavery? Ever since the United States became independent, slavery had caused problems between North and South. The two areas were becoming increasingly different.

Political leaders realized how dangerous the question was. When Missouri applied for admission to the Union as a slave state in 1819, a great debate arose in Congress. Was slavery an evil? Should it be allowed to spread into new areas? Did Congress have the power to restrict it? At that time, there were an equal number of states that permitted slavery and that did not.

Eventually, in 1820–21, a compromise was reached. Missouri was admitted as a slave state, but the balance of slave and free states was kept by admitting Maine as a free state. (Previously Maine had been part of Massachusetts.) A law was also made to forbid slavery in other parts of the Louisiana Purchase north of a certain line. Things quieted down, but the conflict over slavery came back again and again. It eventually threatened the very existence of the United States under the Constitution.

"I take it for granted that the present question is a mere preamble—a title page to a great tragic volume."

John Quincy Adams, son of President John Adams, on the slavery question, in his Diary, 1820

Glossary

agriculture The work of farmers, mostly growing crops and raising livestock for food.

ally A person, group, or country that sides with another in a conflict.

amendment An addition to a formal document—for example, to the United States Consitution.

architect A person who designs buildings.

assembly A group of people gathered together. People elected to make laws in the colonies, and later the states, formed assemblies that were part of local governments.

authority The power to make decisions and rules, or the people who have that power.

bond A certificate promising repayment to a person who has lent money.

confederacy An alliance of several groups that agree to act together and support each other. The Iroquois and Western confederacies were also known as *confederations*.

constitution The basic plan and principles of a government.

Continental Congress The group of men, composed of representatives from the British colonies in North America, that acted as a government for colonists during the American Revolution.

delegate The person chosen to represent others at a meeting or in making decisions.

economic To do with the production and use of goods and services, and the system of money that is used for the flow of good and services.

embargo A government order to stop trade and transport of goods between one country and another.

export To send something abroad to sell or trade. An export is also the thing that is sent, such as tobacco or cotton.

Federalists Supporters of the U.S. Constitution; and the political party that formed around the ideas of Alexander Hamilton in the 1790s.

frontier The edge of something known or settled. In North America, the frontier for white settlers moved as they themselves moved west onto new lands.

import To bring goods into a country. An import is also the thing that is brought in, such as tea or cloth.

indict	To accuse somebody formally of a crime.
integrate	To bring a person or group of people into another, larger group as equals.
interchangeable parts	Pieces of machines that are produced in large numbers and can be replaced if they break.
legislature	An official group of people with the power to make laws.
monarch	A king, queen, emperor, or other ruler who is not elected by votes of the people.
ordinance	A government regulation.
plantation	A farm where crops, such as tobacco or sugarcane, are grown and where the work is done by large teams of workers. In the past, these workers were often slaves.
policy	A plan or way of doing things that is decided on, and then used in managing situations, making decisions, or tackling problems.
radical	A person who favors distinct political, economic, or social changes or reform.
ratify	To approve. For example, the U.S. Senate must ratify treaties before they can go into effect.
repeal	To undo an earlier decision.
Republicans	The political party founded by Thomas Jefferson and James Madison in the 1790s to oppose the policies of Alexander Hamilton and the Federalists; and the political party founded in 1854 to oppose the expansion of slavery.
resolution	A statement that declares the intention or opinion of an official group, such as a government body.
speculator	A person who buys something, risking that it will increase in value and later be sold for more money than was paid for it. This process is called *speculation*.
tariff	A tax on imported goods.
township	An area of United States territory that, in the 1700s, consisted of 36 lots of 640 acres each.
treaty	An agreement reached between two or more groups or countries after discussion and negotiation.
unconstitutional	An action or law not authorized by the Constitution.

Time Line

1781	Articles of Confederation go into effect.
1783	Great Britain recognizes American independence in Treaty of Paris.
1786–87	Shays's Rebellion.
1787	United States Constitution written in Philadelphia.
	Northwest Ordinance passed by Congress.
1788	Constitution ratified.
1789	New United States government under Constitution begins.
	George Washington inaugurated as first president of the United States.
	Judiciary Act passed by Congress.
1791	Bill of Rights becomes part of the Constitution.
	Vermont becomes a state.
	Bank of the United States established.
1792	Kentucky becomes a state.
1793	Eli Whitney invents cotton gin.
	Washington issues Proclamation of Neutrality.
1794	Whiskey Rebellion.
	United States defeats Indians at Battle of Fallen Timbers.
1795	Jay's Treaty with Britain ratified.
	Pinckney's Treaty agreed.
	Treaty of Greenville agreed.
Mid-1790s	Federalist and Republican political parties are formed.
1796	John Adams elected President.
	Tennessee becomes a state.
1797	XYZ Affair.
1798	Alien and Sedition Acts become law.
1798–99	Kentucky and Virginia Resolutions.
1798–1800	Naval conflict with France.
1800	Washington, D.C. becomes capital of the United States.
	Whitney invents interchangeable parts.
	Thomas Jefferson defeats Adams in presidential election.
1801	John Marshall appointed Chief Justice of the United States.
1803	Louisiana Purchase negotiated with France.
	Ohio becomes a state.
	Marbury vs. Madison case gives Supreme Court power of judicial review.

1804–06	Lewis and Clark expedition.
1805	U.S. Navy defeats Tripoli in naval battle.
1807	Robert Fulton builds the steamboat *Clermont*.
	Jefferson signs Embargo Act.
1808	Ban on importation of foreign slaves begins.
	James Madison elected President.
1809	Embargo Act repealed.
1810	United States annexes West Florida.
1811	Indians of Northwest defeated at Battle of Tippecanoe.
1812	War of 1812 begins.
	Louisiana becomes a state.
1813	Battle of the Thames.
	Battle of Lake Erie.
1814	British burn Washington, D.C.
	British defeated by U.S. troops in battles in Canada.
	Hartford Convention.
	Francis Scott Key writes "The Star-Spangled Banner."
	Treaty of Ghent signed.
1815	Andrew Jackson defeats British at Battle of New Orleans.
	Madison declares end of War of 1812.
1815–20	Industrial Revolution takes hold in United States.
1816	Second Bank of the United States chartered by Congress.
	James Monroe elected President.
	Indiana becomes a state.
1817	Rush-Bagot Treaty with Britain.
	Mississippi becomes a state.
	Building starts on Erie Canal (completed 1825).
1818	Convention with Britain.
	Illinois becomes a state.
1819	Financial panic causes economic problems.
	Alabama becomes a state.
	Adams-Onís Treaty with Spain.
1820	Maine becomes a state.
1820–21	Congress passes Missouri Compromise.
1821	Missouri becomes a state.

Further Reading

Gay, Kathlyn and Martin Gay. *War of 1812* (Voices from the Past Series). New York: 21st Century Books, 1995.

Guzzetti, Paula. *White House* (Places in American History Series). Parsippany, NJ: Silver Burdett Press, 1995.

Hansen, Ellen. *Principles of Democracy: The Constitution and the Bill of Rights* (Perspectives on History Series). Carlisle, MA: Discovery Enterprises, 1995.

Kronenwetter, Michael. *Supreme Court of the United States* (American Government in Action Series). Springfield, NJ: Enslow, 1996.

Lindop, Edmund. *Political Parties*. New York: Henry Holt & Co., 1995.

Sakurai, Gail. *The Louisiana Purchase* (Cornerstones of Freedom Series). Danbury, CT: Children's Press, 1998.

Stern, Gary M. *Congress: America's Lawmakers* (Good Citizenship Series). Austin, TX: Raintree Steck-Vaughn, 1997.

Weber, Michael. *Washington, Adams, and Jefferson* (Complete History of Our Presidents Series, Vol. 1). Vero Beach, FL: Rourke Corp., 1996.

White, Deborah Graw. *Let My People Go: African Americans, 1804–1860* (Young Oxford History of African Americans Series). New York: Oxford University Press, 1996.

Websites

The U.S. Constitution Online – USConstitution.net – Offers the text of the Constitution, the Declaration of Independence, the Articles of Confederation, comment/question area, and links to other resources. www.usconstitution.net

Lewis and Clark's Historic Trail – On May 14, 1804, Meriwether Lewis and William Clark set out on an amazing expedition across the Louisiana Territory. Here are maps, journals, and other historic facts. www.lewisclark.net/

Bibliography

Ammon, Harry. *James Monroe and the Quest for National Identity*. New York: McGraw-Hill, 1971.

Commager, Henry Steele, ed. *Documents of American History*. Seventh Edition. New York: Appleton-Century-Crofts, 1963.

Elkins, Stanley, and Eric McKitrick. *The Age of Federalism: The Early American Republic, 1788–1800*. New York: Oxford University Press, 1993.

Fisher, Louis, and Leonard Levy, eds. *Encyclopedia of American Presidents*. New York: Simon & Schuster, 1994.

Malone, Dumas. *Jefferson and the Ordeal of Liberty*. Boston: Little, Brown, 1962.

———. *Jefferson the President: First Term, 1801–1805*. Boston: Little, Brown, 1970.

———. *Jefferson the President: Second Term, 1805–1809*. Boston: Little, Brown, 1974.

Middlekauf, Robert. *The Glorious Cause: The American Revolution, 1763–1789*. New York: Oxford University Press, 1982.

Miller, John C. *The Federalist Era, 1789–1801*. New York: Harper, 1960.

Morgan, Edmund S. *The Birth of the Republic, 1763–1789*. Chicago: University of Chicago Press, 1963.

Rutland, Robert F., ed. *James Madison and the American Nation, 1751–1836: An Encyclopedia*. New York: Simon & Schuster, 1994.

Smith, Page. *The Shaping of America: A People's History of the Young Republic*. New York: McGraw-Hill, 1980.

Index

Page numbers in *italics* indicate maps; numbers in **bold** indicate illustrations.

Adams, John, 16, 27, 28, 47–48, 50, 51, 76, 77
   as president, 50, 51, 52, 54, 55, 58, 63
Adams, John Quincy, 76, 80, 87
Adams-Onís Treaty, 79, 80
agriculture, 6, 38, 82
Alabama, 79, 86
Alien and Sedition Acts, 52–53
American Revolution, 6, 7, 8, 9, 12, 14, 18, 21, 33, 35, 36, 40, 43, 46, 65, 77, 78
Antifederalists, 24, 26
Appalachian Mountains, 6, 9, 11, 39, *39*, 40, 41, 86
Articles of Confederation, 8–9, 17, 24, 27
attorney general, 33

Baltimore, 73, *75*, 80, 82
banks, 48, 84–85
   National, 37–38, **38**, 46, 77, 84
Barbary States, 63
battles,
   in Canada, 70, 72, 73, *75*,
   with French, 52, **52**
   naval, 52, **52**, 63, 72
   in New Orleans, 75–76, *75*,
   with Tripoli, 63
   in the South, 71, *75*,
   in the West, 39, 40, 43, 69, 70, *75*
Bill of Rights, 24, 26, 30–32
black people, 6, 49, 62, 69, 86
   see also slaves
Bonaparte, Napoleon, 59, 60, 72, 73
bonds, 35, 36, 37, 82
Britain, 6, 9, 28, 43, 44, 45, 48, 49, 51, 56, 59, 64, 65, 68, 78, 79, 80
   war with U.S., 64, 68, 71–77, 81

British
   colonies, 6, 8, 12
   in the West, 11, 41, 43, 44, 69
British army, 43, 72
   burns Washington, D.C., 34, 54, 73, 74
   in Canada, 70, 72
   in War of 1812, 34, 54, 70, 72–73, 74, 75, 76
British navy, 43, 44, 64, 72
Burr, Aaron, 36, 51, 55, 63, 65

Cabinet, 33, **33**, 34, 36, 45, 81
Canada, 6, 39, 43, 60, 65, 68, 70, 72, 73, *75*, 79, 80
canals, 86
Capitol building, 34, 57, 73
cities, growth of, 82, **82**, 84, 86
Civil War, 34, 62, 66, 67
Clark, William, 61, **61**
Clay, Henry, 18, 62, 68, **69**, 74, 76
Congress, 8, 9, 10, 11, 12, 14, 16, 17, 19, 27, 28, 30, 32, 34, 58, 60, 61, 62, 67, 71, 77, 85, 87
   House of Representatives, 19, 20, 21, 26, 27, 30, 56, **81**
   powers of, 20, 23, 35, 37
   Senate, 19, 20, 23, 27, 29, 30, 44
   see also national government
Connecticut, 25, 39, *75*, 75
Constitution, the, 16, 19–21, **22**, 23, 24, 27, 28, 29, 30, 32, 38, 47, 48, 55, 58, 60, 75, 81, 87
   amendments to, 21, 26, 30, 31, 32
   checks and balances, 23–24, 87
   ratification of, 24–26, **25**, 27, 28, 33, 36
Constitutional Convention, 16–21, **19**, 23, 24
   delegates, 16, 17, 19, 20, 21, 23, 36

Continental Congress, 8, 34, 46
Convention of 1818, 80
cotton gin, 83, 84, **84**
courts
   national, 9, 20, 30, 32, 33
   state, 13, 14, 32
   see also Supreme Court
Creek War, 71, *75*

debt
   national, 12, 35, 36, 37, 44, 58
   personal, 12–13, 14
   states, 35, 37
Declaration of Independence, 21, 33
Delaware, 14, 25, 39, 75, 83
Democratic party, 56, 66
Democratic-Republicans, 56
Detroit, 39, 40, 72, *75*

economy, 6, 7, 11, 35, 37, 82, 84, 86
education, 15, 49, 57, 67
elections, 20, 21, 26, 27, 50–51, 56, 63, 82
   of 1800, 26, 36, 50, 53, 55–56, **55**, 57
Embargo Act, 65, 66, 68, 77
Era of Good Feelings, 79, 87
Europe, 6, 7, 43, 52, 73, 77

Fallen Timbers, Battle of, 39, 40, 43, 70
farmers, 12, 13, 38, 41, 48, 63, 82
Federalists, 24, 25, 26, 47–48, **48**, 49, **49**, 50, 51, 52, 53, 55, 56, 57, 58, 74–75, 79, 82
Florida, 6, 39, 59, 60, 68, 69, *75*, 79, 80
foreign affairs, 8, 11, 29, 32, 35, 43–45, 46, 47, 48, 49, 51–52, 59, 63–64, 68, 78, 79–80
France, 6, 7, 12, 33, 43, 44, 48, 49, 59, 64, 65, 68, 72, 77
   crisis with, 51–52, 55

Franklin, Benjamin, 16, **17**
French navy, 43, 44, **52**
French Revolution, 43–44
Fulton, Robert, 86

Gallatin, Albert, 75, 76
Genêt, Edmond Charles, 44
Georgia, 6, 15, 25, 39, *75*

Hamilton, Alexander, 16, 25, **25**, 26, 28, 33, **33**, 35–39, **36**, 41, 42, 45, 47, 48, 51, 55, 56, 58, 65, 77
Harrison, William Henry, 69, 72
Hartford Convention, 75
Henry, Patrick, 16, 25, 26
Horseshoe Bend, Battle of, 71, *75*, 76

Illinois, 11, 79, 85, 86
impressment, 43, 44, **44**, 64, 72, 77, 78
Indiana, 11, 69, 79, 86
Indiana Territory, 41, 69, *75*
Industrial Revolution, 82–84
Iroquois Confederacy, 39, 40

Jackson, Andrew, 56, 71, **71**, 76
Jay, John, 25, 33, 44
Jay's Treaty, 44, 45, 51
Jefferson, Thomas, 10, 11, 15, 16, 18, 24, 33, **33**, 36, 37, 38, 39, 45, 47, 48, 49, 50, 51, 53, 56, 66–67, 78, 87
    election of, 50, **55**, 55, 56, 57
    as president, 50, 54, 57–58, 59–60, 61, 62–64, 65, 66 , 72, 74, 82
Judiciary Act, 32

Kentucky, 39, 41, *75*, 86
Kentucky Resolutions, 53, 59
Key, Francis Scott, 80
King, Rufus, 16, 79
Knox, Henry, 33, **33**

labor unions, 84
Lafitte, Jean, 76

Lake Erie, Battle of, 72, **73**, *75*
laws, 9, 17, 18, 20, 21, 23, 32, 42, 52, 53, 58–59, 62, 63, 64, 65, 68, 77, 80, 87
Lewis, Meriwether, 61, **61**
Lewis and Clark Expedition, 60, 61, **61**
Lincoln, Abraham, 56, 67
Livingston, Robert, 59
Louisiana, 39, 59, 60, *60*, 62
    as a state, 60, 75, 86
Louisiana Purchase, 59–60, *60*, 62, 66, 69, 75, 78, 80, 82, 87

Madison, Dolley, 18, 74
Madison, James, 14, 16, 17, 18, 25, 26, 30, **30**, 39, 48, 49, 53, 56, 62, 64, 79
    as president, 57, 68, 69, 71, 72, 74, 77, 78, 82
Maine, 39, 73, *75*, 79, 86, 87
manufacturing industries, 38, 39, 65, 77, 82–84, **82, 83**
Marbury vs. Madison, 58–59
Marshall, John, 58, **58**, 59, 82
Maryland, 14, 15, 25, 34, 39, *75*, 85
Massachusetts, 12, 13, **13**, 14, 25, 39, 73, *75*, *75*, 86, 87
Michigan, 11
Mississippi, 79, 86
Mississippi River, 6, 9, *10*, 11, 39, *39*, 41, 45, 59, 60, *60*, 61, 69, *75*, *75*
Mississippi Territory, 41, 62, *75*
Missouri, 60, 79, 86, 87
money, 8, 9, 12, 20, 35, 36, 37, 46, **46**
Monroe, James, 59, 62, 78, **78**, 87
    as president, 57, 78–79, 80, 82
Monroe Doctrine, 78

Nantucket Island, 73, *75*
national government, 7, 8, 28, 29, 32, 35, 37, 39, 45, 46, 47, *75*, 87
    creation, 16, 17, 18, 19–20
    departments, 30, 32, 33, 34
    executive branch, 18, 20, 30, 32, 33, 58, 81

judicial branch, 18, 20, 23, 32, 58
legislative branch, 18–19, 20, 58
powers, 7, 8–9, 14, 17, 18, 20, 23, 24, 38, 42, 48, 49, 58, 66, 81
secretaries, 33, **33**
    see also Congress
Native Americans, 6, 11, 39, 40, 43, 49, 60, 61, 69, 71, 77, 86, 87
    conflict with white people, 40, 41, 43, 69–71, 72
    lands, 39, 40, 49, 63, 69, 81
    relations with white people, 35, 61, 63, 69, 70, 71
    treaties, 29, 40, **71**
    in War of 1812, 70, 72
Naturalization Act, 53
New England, 34, 48, 51, 66, 75, 83
New Hampshire, 14, 25, 39, *75*, *75*
New Jersey, 14, 25, 34, 39, *75*, *75*
New Orleans, 11, 39, 45, 59, 60, *60*, 62
    Battle of, 75–76, *75*
New York, 12, 14, 15, 25, 26, 39, 40, 51, 73, *75*, *75*, 86
New York City, 6, 27, **27**, 34, 82
North Carolina, 6, 14, 15, 26, *39*, *75*
Northwest, the, 10–11, *10*, 11, 39, *39*, 40, 41, 69–71
Northwest Ordinance, 10–11

Ohio, 11, 39, 40, 41, *75*, 86

Pakenham, Edward, 76
Pennsylvania, 12, 14, 18, 25, 34, 39, 40, 41, 42, 51, *75*
Perry, Oliver, 72, **73**
Philadelphia, 6, 8, 14, 16, 34, 46, 54, 82
Pinckney, Charles Cotesworth, 16, 55
Pinckney, Thomas, 45, 50, 59
Pinckney's Treaty, 45, 59
Pittsburgh, 42, **82**, 83
political parties, 47, 56, 82
post office, 8–9, 11, 32
president, 29
    appointments by, 20, 23, 33
    election, 20, 26, 27, 75
    powers, 20, 23, 29, 66, 81–82

Proclamation of Neutrality, 44
Prophetstown, 69, *75*

Randolph, Edmund, 16, 17, 33, **33**
Report on Manufactures, 38
Report on a National Bank, 37
Report on the Public Credit, 35
Republicans, 47, 48–49, **48**, **49**,
 50, 51, 52, 53, 55, 56, 57, 58,
 63, 65, 66, 68, 75, 82
Rhode Island, 12, 14, 16, 26, 39,
 75, *75*
Rush-Bagot Treaty, 79–80, *79*

Sacagawea, **61**
St. Louis, 60, *60*, 61
Shays, Daniel, 13, 14
Shays's Rebellion, **13**, 14
slavery, 11, 21, 23, 49, 56, 62, 66,
 67, 84, 87
slaves, 6, 21, 23, **23**, 28, 43, 44,
 49, 62, 68, **84**, 86
South, the, 23, 48, 49, 51, 62, 72,
 79, 84, 87
South Carolina, 25, 39, 75, 86
Southwest, the, *10*, 39, *39*
Spain, 11, 43, 45, 59, 78, 80
Spanish territory, 6, 11, 39, 41, 44,
 45, 59, 60, 61, 68, 75, 79, 80
speculators, 9, 36, 37
"Star-Spangled Banner," 80, **80**
state governments, 8, 18, 32, 53, 87
 powers, 7, 17, 20, 24, 48, 53, 59, 81
states, 8, 87
 elections, 21, 26, 27
 new, 9, 11, 20, 39, 41, 60, 75,
 79, 86, 87
 ratification of Constitution, 24,
 25–26

states' rights, 53, 59, 66
steamboats, 85–86
Supreme Court, 20, 32, 33, 58, 59, 82

taxes, 9, 12, 14, 17, 20, 35, 37, 38,
 51, 52, 53, 58, 74
 on imports, 12, 20, 35, 38–39, 77

on whiskey, 41, 42
Tecumseh, 69, 70, 71, 72
Tennessee, 15, 39, 41, 75, 86
Tenskwatawa, 69, 70, **70**
Texas, 60, *79*, 80
Thames, Battle of the, 70, 72, *75*
Tippecanoe, Battle of, 69, 70, *75*
trade, 12, 14, 41, 72
 between states, 9, 11
 foreign, 6, **7**, 11, 39, 43, 44, 64,
 68, 82, 83
 fur, 11, 43
 limits on, 12, 43, 65, 68
 regulation, 17, 20
 slave, 23, 62
transportation, 85–86, **85**, 87
treaties, 6, 11, 20, 23, 29, 40, 44,
 45, 51, 52, 59, 60, 70, 71, 76,
 77, 79–80
Treaty of Ghent, 76, **76**, 77
Treaty of Greenville, 40, 70
Treaty of Paris, 6, 11
Tripoli, 63, **64**
Turner, Nat, 62
turnpikes, 85, **85**, 86

United States of America
 boundaries, 9, *10*, 39, *39*, 60,
 60, *75*, 77, *79*, 80
 capital, 27, 34, **34**, 54
 population, 6, 10, 21, 39–40,
 60, 86, 87
 territory, 6, 9–11, *10*, 39, 40,
 43, 60, *60*, 62, 68, *75*, 79, 80,
 85, 86, 87
United States Army, 40, 41, 42,
 51, 52, 67
 in Canada, 70, 72
 in the South, 71
 in War of 1812, 72, 73, 76
 in the West, 69
United States Navy, 51, 52, **52**,
 58, 63, 64, **64**, 72, **73**
universities, 15, **15**

Vermont, 15, 39, 75, *75*, 86
vice president, 20, 26, 27

Virginia, 14, 25, 26, 39, 62, 75
Virginia Plan, 17, 18, 19
Virginia Resolutions, 53, 59
voting, 8, 17, 19, 20, 21, 26, 27,
 49, 82

War Hawks, 68, **69**, 71
War of 1812, 34, 54, *75*, 77, 78,
 79, 80, 81
 in Canada, 72, 73
 capture of Detroit, 72
 in Maryland, 73
 in Massachusetts, 73
 in New Orleans, 72–73
 in New York, 73
 opposition to, 74–75
 peace negotiations, 76–77
 support for, 72
Washington, D. C., 15, 34, **34**, 54,
 54, 57, 73, 74, *75*
Washington, George, 14, 15, 18,
 23, 26, 28, 36, 51, 66
 at Constitutional Convention,
 16, 17, **19**
 Farewell Address, 46, 47
 inauguration, 27, **27**, 30
 as military hero, 28
 as president, 27–29, 33, **33**, 34,
 37, 38, 40, 41, 42, 44, 45–46,
 47, 48, 50, 63, 79, 82
Washington, Martha, 28
Wayne, Anthony, 40
Webster, Noah, 15
West, the, 9–11, *10*, 35, 39–42, *39*,
 43, 72, 79, 80, 84
 cities, **82**
 division of, 10, 11
 settlers, 9, 10, 11, 39–41, 49, 81
Western Confederacy, 39, 40, 69
West Indies, 12, 23, 43, 44
West Point Military Academy, 67, **67**
Whigs, 56
Whiskey Rebellion, 42, **42**, 82
White House, 34, **54**, 54, 73, 74
Whitney, Eli, 83, 84
Wisconsin, 11, 69